Doggie Doings

in Jackson Hole, Wyoming

and Teton Valley, Idaho

A Complete Reference

Judy F. Eddy, Editor

Two Mountain Press
Jackson Hole, Wyoming

Two Mountain Press
PO Box 11822
Jackson WY 83002

ISBN 0-**9679550-0-9**

ACKNOWLEDGMENTS

All photos are by the author or printed with permission by the photographers.

Research provided by the following:

HIKES: Lorene and "Chief;" Barbara and "Holden," "Holly," "Phoebe" (deceased); Kim and "Max"; Susan and "Bayou"; Sophie and "Dipper," "Sam," "Rhoger," "Popcorn," "Bo" (deceased); Bea and "Lola" (deceased); Carol and "McKenzie"; Ann and "Pico," "Captain"; Kathy and "Chancey"; and "Toby"

DIRECTORY OF SERVICES: Julie Mossman

REVIEWS and invaluable suggestions provided by Lori Findlay, Dan Forman DVM, Susan Fox, Lisa Goldoftas, Carolyn Gunn DVM, Susan McElroy, Kim McGregor, Erica Periman DVM, Jonathan Schechter, and Barbara Trachtenberg. Any errors are the responsibility of the editor.

TO TOBY
(the Wonderful Weimaraner)

whose love and companionship inspired this project

and TO MY SPONSORS

whose financial support allowed me to print the book

Black Diamond Vacation Rentals and Real Estate (see pp 136, 150)
The Charles Engelhard Foundation
The Hairball Hotel (see pg 125)
Patrick and Ann Smith
Spring Creek Veterinary Hospital (see pp 126, 131, 146, 152)

Printed in the United States of America

Table of Contents

13 Directory of Dog Services

14 Musings About Dogs

1 Why This Book?

by Judy F. Eddy

This book is for pet owners and their dogs who are privileged to live in Jackson Hole, as well as for those who are just visiting. Jackson Hole is a special place for dogs, and has frequently been called "Dog Heaven on Earth." The people of the valley, the incredible natural surroundings, the four seasons — all combine to make Jackson Hole special. Approximately 97% of Teton County is public land in the form of national parks, national forests, the National Elk Refuge, Bureau of Land Management (BLM) land, and conservancy holdings. A large portion of this land (e.g., the national forests) has few restrictions on dogs.

Many people who live here have dogs. An unofficial count of dogs in Teton County reveals more than 9000 (plus another 3000 in Teton Valley Idaho). This equates to approximately one dog for every household.

It is often difficult for both newcomers and the thousands of visitors to Jackson Hole to know exactly where they can take their dogs for a long dayhike or even a short 20-minute walk. This book describes the Jackson Hole Community Pathways system, and 28 dog-friendly hikes and walks. It includes a description of the hike lengths and vistas for you, the availability of water for your dog, and the likelihood of encountering wildlife. These hikes are not the only ones you can take with your dog; they are listed because they are easily accessible, are less than 10 miles in length, and are some favorites of our local dogs.

In addition, you will find other dog-related information in this book. A very important chapter presents the rules and regulations relating to dog ownership in Teton County. Another chapter describes what the local dogs do for fun and for work. Information about the animal shelters on both sides of the Teton Mountain Range, about responsibilities of dog ownership and about hiking with your dog (including what to do if you or your dog encounter wildlife) is included. You will also find important information about caring for your dog in a natural disaster, and about first aid while hiking with your dog. What to do if you lose your dog is another chapter. The Directory of Dog Services lists addresses and phone numbers for dog-friendly lodging (for guests and for residents: bed and breakfasts, campgrounds, condominiums, motels, guest ranches, property management, resorts, vacation rentals); doggie boarding, daycare and doggie sitters;

veterinarians; trainers; groomers; suppliers; sled dog tours; and who to contact if you want to get involved in any of the canine capers described in the chapter on what our dogs do. The book ends with musings about hunting dogs, dealing with the death of your dog, and concludes with some humor.

If you have a dog, whatever your needs, they are covered in this book.

DISCLAIMER: All information was current at the time of printing to the best of my knowledge, but no guarantees beyond that can be made. If you find that a "dog friendly" location listed in this book has changed its policy, please inform the editor. If you have additions or corrections to the book, please contact the editor for inclusion in future editions. Two Mountain Press, PO Box 11822, Jackson WY 83002 (307) 733-9167; judy@dog.com

(The editor uses the male pronoun for the dogs but this is not intended to slight our female dogs -- it is for ease of use only.)

"A dog is a smile and a wagging tail. What is in between doesn't matter much."
                    Clara Ortega

2   Dog Rules and Regulations in Jackson Hole

by Corie Rybak

Because of the distribution of public and private lands in Jackson Hole, a number of different government entities in Teton County play a role in dog regulations and animal control. Jackson Hole is a very special place, one that people enjoy in a variety of ways. Respecting and obeying these basic rules preserves the natural environment and makes life more pleasant for everyone.

Each area in which you play might have restrictions on how your dog can accompany you. In addition, the Town of Jackson has specific ordinances relating to animal control and care. With a few exceptions, Teton County's regulations are essentially the same. Some residential areas might have additional conditions attached to pet ownership. Whether you are just visiting Teton County or the valley is your home, you should know about and comply with these rules and regulations. They outline proper treatment of animals and ensure public safety and good neighbor relations. If you see anyone violating these ordinances, file a complaint with local law enforcement.

For the most part, as a pet owner, use common sense: Do not allow your dog to behave in a manner that might annoy or interfere with another's enjoyment. Remember, your actions will affect the availability of dog access not only for yourself but for all other dogs and their owners.

Public Recreation Lands

National Parks

Dogs are allowed in both Yellowstone and Grand Teton National Parks but must remain on a leash with a maximum length of 6 feet. Dogs are not allowed on any trails, in public buildings or visitor centers, on ranger-led activities, or in the backcountry. This means that they cannot be taken more than 50 feet from any roadway. You cannot leave your dog unattended or tied to any object. In Yellowstone, your dog is not allowed in the thermal basins. Even with this restriction, local veterinarians usually treat at least one dog a year for severe thermal burns. Your dog is allowed in campgrounds, but he must be leashed. Please be considerate of other campers by keeping your dog quiet and picking up any messes he leaves. Pet regulations are strictly enforced in both parks and fines are imposed for violations.

National Forests

The Bridger-Teton and Targhee National Forests are the most dog-friendly public lands in the area. With the exception of campgrounds where the dogs must remain on a leash that measures no more than 6 feet, there are no rules regarding the restraint of dogs.

However, this freedom must not be abused! Certain areas receive intensive use. Be considerate of others so that negative encounters are kept to a minimum and the Forest Service will not be forced to take an active regulatory role against dogs in the future. Dog droppings and unruly dogs are two issues the Forest Service is grappling with. Do your part; clean up after your dog and be sure that he is under control.

In the winter, certain areas of the National Forests are off limits due to Wildlife Winter Range Closures. Please respect these closures.

National Elk Refuge

Dogs are restricted to the road and can be shot if seen running the range.

Town Parks

No dog is allowed in any Town park, including the Jackson Town Square and all ball parks. Violations can result in a minimum $50 citation.

Jackson Hole Community Pathways

The Pathways system is a multiple-use amenity. One section of the pathways requires that your dog be leashed. Please be aware of this area (it is well posted), and respect the request. Some people would like to see dogs prohibited entirely, so the more cooperative dog owners are, the better for all. Much of the Pathways sections border private property; please show respect to the adjoining homeowners.

Use the Mutt Mitts that are provided to keep the paths clean for other users. Since the pathways are patrolled, violators can be cited under care and control ordinances.

Any Lands Within the State

State statute provides that dogs observed harassing, running, or injuring big game animals can be destroyed immediately by any law enforcement or peace officer. Please realize that wildlife can be encountered along the county pathways, or even in town, especially during the winter months.

State statutes also provide that any dog running livestock (without permission of the livestock owner) can be killed immediately. Alternatively, the livestock owner can press charges against the dog owner.

Town and County Regulations
Care
Dogs shall be provided with good and sufficient food and water, proper shelter, protection from the weather, and veterinary care as needed.

Dogs shall not be beaten, cruelly ill-treated, tormented, or otherwise abused, nor shall the owner abandon any animal. Cruelty can include leaving a dog locked in a car during the warm summer months. Any such cruelty or inhumane treatment of an animal can result in a citation with a $500 bond. This is the amount you will have to pay to avoid going to court.

If you live within the town boundaries, you cannot keep or maintain more than two dogs over the age of three months on your property.

Every female dog in heat shall be confined in a secure enclosure.

Under Control vs At-Large
Dogs must be "under control" at all times. This means that your dog must be under physical restraint (on a leash), or in your presence and subject to and responsive to your verbal command. A dog is not under control if he is running at large or unrestrained in the streets, along the sidewalks, or on any school ground, playground, park, or place of public amusement or recreation.

Your dog is "at large" if he is off your premises and not under control or restraint.

You are not allowed to tie your dog to any mailbox, post or other structure that is next to a public doorway or sidewalk if doing so would interfere with pedestrian traffic or impede the entrance to any building frequented by the general public.

Public Nuisance
Exercise proper care and control of your dog to prevent him from becoming a public nuisance. A nuisance dog includes any noisy dog; vicious dog; or a dog who chews, tears, digs or scratches, litters or soils, destroys or in any other manner injures public or private property, real or personal.

Excessive, continued or untimely barking, molesting of passersby, chasing of vehicles, habitual attacking of other domestic animals, or trespassing on private property so as to damage property (which includes leaving dog poops in someone's yard), can be deemed a nuisance.

Vicious or Biting Dog

No dog of fierce, dangerous or vicious propensity shall be allowed to run at large. If any such dog is running at large and cannot be safely taken up and impounded, he can be killed by a police officer, in the interest of public safety.

Any dog who is believed to have rabies, has been bitten by an animal suspected of having rabies, or has bitten any person, shall be impounded and quarantined for 14 days. At the end of the quarantine, the dog must be inspected by a licensed veterinarian who will authorize release or disposal of the dog. All costs of impoundment, board and veterinary services must be paid by the owner prior to the release of the dog.

Violation of Any Care and Control or Restraint Provision

Any person violating any care and control or restraint provision of the Town Ordinances is guilty of a misdemeanor and subject to the following fines:

1st conviction: $25 - $750
2nd conviction: $50 - $750
3rd conviction: $75 - $750
4th conviction: permit to own a dog can be revoked.
(This permit is the license you are required to have for your dog.)

Violation of Teton County regulations can result in a citation with an initial $100 maximum fine.

Unrestrained dogs can be picked up and impounded in the Animal Shelter, where the impound fee is currently $20 (plus $8 for every night after the first). Proof of rabies vaccination must be provided or the vaccination must be paid for in advance. Your dog must be licensed prior to his being released.

If the owner cannot readily be determined (because the dog has no license or other identification), he will be held for six days and then be placed for adoption or otherwise disposed of.

Licensing

Any dog older than six months of age must have a dog license. This license is to be renewed every January. The license requires a valid certificate of rabies vaccination.

You can get a license at the Animal Shelter for either the Town of Jackson or Teton County, depending on where you live. You can also get a Town license at the Town Hall on East Pearl Avenue. For County dogs, you can get a license at the County Administration Office (Treasurer's Department) on Willow Street.

Licenses shall be worn at all times when the dog is off the owner's premises.

Even though dogs in Jackson Hole must be licensed, a survey of the veterinarians for the number of their dog clients and a count of dog licenses issued revealed that only 10% of resident dogs are currently licensed.

Any dog belonging to a nonresident of Teton County must have a valid license or permit issued by another municipal corporation, as well as proof of current rabies vaccination; if not, the dog can be impounded. Not having a valid dog permit can result in a $25 citation.

DOG. n. A kind of additional or subsidiary deity designed to catch the overflow and surplus of the world's worship.
Ambrose Bierce
The Devil's Dictionary (1911)

3   Responsibilities of Dog Ownership

by Judy F. Eddy

This chapter is important for all dog owners.

When regulations require that your dog be "on leash" (e.g., in town and in certain other locations), please abide by that — it makes it easier for others who have dogs, as well as more pleasant for those who do not.

All dogs residing in Teton County, including the Town of Jackson, must be licensed. The license requires proof of rabies vaccination.

Your dog is not allowed to bite anyone, whether human, canine, feline, or others. Your dog is not allowed to chase livestock or wildlife. Law enforcement officials can legally kill your dog if he is seen chasing these animals.

Common courtesy is always required when you have a dog. Although dogs love people, the reverse is not always true. Do not allow your dog to do anything to aggravate the situation.

If you know your dog is aggressive, put him on a leash. Warn any approaching dog owners to keep their dog away because your dog might fight. Conversely, if you see a dog on a leash or see a person putting a dog on a leash at your approach, keep your dog under control and away. That is a signal to you that your dog is not welcome to approach that dog. He might be ill, he might be recovering from surgery, he might be aggressive, or he might be timid — be respectful.

Keep identification on your dog. Even the best behaved dogs wander off or get lost. This is especially important for visitors to the valley. Your dog's identification tag with your home address and phone number is useless if there is no one at home because you are visiting the national parks. For a few dollars, you can make a tag as you travel, putting your travel locations and contact phone numbers on your dog. There are quick (5-minute), easy-to-make identification tags that can be used as you travel. These tags are available from Teton County PAL at (307) 733-9167. They are cute, inexpensive, and you can put on it any information you want.

Spaying and Neutering

In just 6 years, one female dog and her offspring can produce 67,000 animals!!! Thus, responsible ownership involves spaying or neutering your dog.

Our local veterinarians encourage the spaying and neutering of pets to stop overpopulation, and they charge about half of their cost in hopes that more pet owners will opt for the procedure for their dogs.

A spayed or neutered dog will live a longer and healthier life. Neutering a male dog by six months of age prevents testicular cancer, prostate disease and hernias. A big advantage in neutering a male dog is behavioral; testosterone reduction can reduce misdirected and territorial behavior. Spaying a female dog helps prevent pyometra (a pus-filled uterus) and breast cancer. Having the surgery before the first heat offers the best protection from these diseases. Treatment of pyometra requires hospitalization, intravenous fluids, antibiotics and spaying. Breast cancer can be fatal in about 50% of female dogs. Ovarian and uterine diseases affect the majority of unspayed females as they age.

Although commonly believed, it is a myth that a neutered or spayed dog will become fat and lazy. Lack of exercise and overfeeding are the cause. Spayed and neutered dogs tend to live an average of two to three years longer than those who are not.

Humane societies say that about 30% of the people who adopt pets fail to honor the adoption contract, which requires that the animal be spayed or neutered. Failure to honor the contract means that already crowded shelters become more crowded.

Under Control

Another requirement of dog ownership involves having your dog under control. This means that your dog cannot run loose in neighborhoods, potentially scare or bother children and adults, or do his business on others' property. If you know that your dog is not obedient under voice control, do keep him on a leash. There is one section of the Jackson Hole Community Pathways on which dogs MUST be leashed.

Wandering and roaming dogs can get hit by automobiles. Most of these dogs are unneutered males. A male can smell a female dog in heat from a distance of up to three miles. These facts should provide the impetus for you to spay and neuter your dogs. Do not let your dog become a statistic. Good dog ownership involves a well trained dog.

Dog Poop

Unscooped dog poop is a major reason dogs are banned from parks, apartments, and other locations. The 9000 or so dogs in Jackson Hole are responsible for approximately 3-1/2 tons of dog poop every year!

Because any one dog owner represents all other dog owners, it is important that all are responsible. Dog droppings are more obnoxious to some people than are discarded beer cans, paper wrappers, and cigarette butts.

Not only is dog poop offensive to humans, but it can be dangerous to dogs. Your dog is at danger from intestinal parasites such as worms and viral infections such as parvo from dog poop deposited by an infected dog.

If you are walking your dog in a neighborhood and he poops on someone's nicely manicured lawn, pick it up with a plastic bag. If your dog poops in the middle of a trail when you are hiking, use sticks, twigs, a ski pole, or whatever, to move it off the trail. Even better, train him to go off the trail to do his business.

If you use the Jackson Hole Community Pathways system, you are responsible for cleaning your dog's poop. The Town of Jackson and Friends of Pathways have set up a program to help with the potential problem. Mutt Mitt dispensers and trash receptacles are located along the Russ Garaman and School Trails of the Jackson Hole Community Pathways System. Mutt Mitts are plastic bags that allow dog owners to conveniently pick up their pet's waste, and deposit it in the trash receptacles along the trail.

Signs are posted to educate dog owners about the Pathway dog rules. So that dog walkers can continue to use the Pathways, please obey the regulations.

Commitment

It has been estimated that 52 million dogs in the US are family pets. However, millions of them are euthanized in US shelters each year. As many as 61% of all dogs entering shelters are killed, and as many as 25% of all dogs in shelters are purebreds.

ALONE AGAIN

I wish someone would tell me what it is that I've done wrong.
Why I have to stay chained up and left alone so long.
They seemed so glad to have me when I came here as a pup.
There were so many things we'd do while I was growing up.
They couldn't wait to train me as a companion and a friend.
And told me how they'd never fear being left alone again.
The children said they'd feed me and brush me every day.
They'd play with me and walk me if only I could stay.
But now the family "hasn't time"; they often say I shed.
They do not even want me in the house, not even to be fed.
The children never walk me; they always say "Not now."
I wish that I could please them; won't somebody tell me how?
All I had, you see, was love. I wish they would explain
Why they said they wanted me, then left me on a chain?

Anonymous

4   Why Train Your Dog?

by Judy F. Eddy

Obedience training is one of the most important aspects of raising your dog.

A well trained dog is by far a happier dog! Why? Because a trained dog requires fewer restrictions. The more reliable your dog, the more freedom your dog can be given. For example, many local stores and businesses that normally will not allow dogs on their premises might make an exception for a puppy or a dog that will heel nicely by an owner's side, or will do a sit-stay or down-stay without hesitation.

Moreover, because a well mannered, obedience-trained dog is both appreciated and welcome, your pet will receive more attention and interaction from passersby and visitors than will an ill-mannered dog. Do not assume that all people will like your dog. However, if he has good manners in public, more people will appreciate him.

Training strengthens the bond between you and your dog. It builds communication, understanding, mutual respect, and subtly but effectively demonstrates that you are the leader of the pack (or the "alpha").

Obedience training can save your dog's life. When you read in Chapter 9 about the wildlife you might encounter on your hikes, you will become aware of the necessity of having your dog under control. It can mean the difference between life and death for both you and your dog.

A well trained dog will be less likely to cause an accident to a horseback rider or to an older person or child on a hiking trail.

The consequences of an untrained dog extend beyond just your dog. When you allow your dog to misbehave, everyone suffers. You, because you live with your dog; your dog, because everyone is down on him for misbehaving; your neighbors, because living next to a difficult dog is no one's idea of fun; and ultimately every dog owner, because each incident where your dog creates a nuisance increases anti-dog sentiment, and contributes to the likelihood that tough legal restrictions will be placed on all dogs. Obedience training benefits everyone.

A well behaved, obedience-trained dog is a pleasure to own because he can go virtually anywhere without being a risk or a nuisance to others. And you definitely want your dog to exhibit appropriate behavior in a crowd, to be reliable around children, and to not threaten other dogs or passersby. When you walk with him in town on his leash, it will be a pleasure for him as well as for you and those you encounter. Also, a well mannered dog will display good manners when you have guests in your home.

Once your dog has been trained, your work is not over. Realize that his obedience training was most probably done under controlled conditions, and on a leash. The purpose of training your dog is to be able to transfer the commands to the real world. As you and your dog interact with others, it is imperative that your dog obey you. You want him to be reliable and to listen to you in a variety of other situations. He must obey you when he is out, as well as he does at home.

When you are hiking with your dog, the distraction level increases. There are other people, other dogs, horseback riders, bicyclists, deer and moose, as well as other smaller animals, such as squirrels and porcupines. If you practice his training along the trails before and while he encounters these distractions, your dog will realize that obedience is required in these situations as well.

You cannot train your dog to react properly around a horse without a horse being present, or a moose without a moose being present. However, if he is under your control and used to obeying you when you are together on the trail at other times, you will be able to feel confident that he will obey you when you do come upon a horse or moose.

It is important to respect the horseback riders and the wildlife because they are the grassroots of the Jackson Hole west that we love so much.

It is your responsibility to prepare your dog for all expected encounters. The hikes describe what you might expect: other people, horseback riders, bicyclists, or wildlife. For example, if you take your dog on the levee along the Snake River, do not let him disturb anyone fishing in the river or the ponds. It will be up to you to be sure he does not dash into the water just as a fisherman is ready to make the catch of the day. Take your dog downstream or to a different pond.

Some clever dogs realize that your control is different when you are on skis or a bicycle, or running rather than walking. Work with your dog so that he knows that he must obey you at all times.

Practice training your dog from a distance. You can use a 30-foot leash so that you have a way to control him. If your dog is three feet from you and 37 feet from a squirrel or another dog, you have a greater likelihood of getting your dog to respond to your command than if your dog is 37 feet from you and three feet from the squirrel or the other dog. Gradually increase the distance between you and your dog as you give him commands. Realize that "objects of attraction" will be just that. *Your role is to get him to realize that YOU are a better attraction.*

Different environments might affect your dog's demeanor. Do not expect him to automatically generalize the meaning of a given command in every environment or context. Your dog might walk sedately with you on a sidewalk, but once you get on a forest trail, he might bolt after a squirrel. Practice your basic obedience commands in these different surroundings.

Take the time to teach the basic commands in as many different situations as you can imagine. In this way, walking or hiking with your dog will be pleasurable for you, him, and others. The ultimate goal is for your dog to have good manners in public, whether walking through town or hiking on the trails, or just at home.

"The dog is man's best friend. He has a tail on one end. Up in front he has teeth. And four legs underneath."
Ogden Nash

5 Canine Capers, or What Do the Dogs Do?

by Judy F. Eddy

Abundant activities exist for dogs in Teton County. They work, they play, they hunt, they compete, they bring joy, they heal, they find, they save lives, they learn, and they give their undying love.

This chapter gives an overview of organized activities in which you and your dog can participate. If you are at least 9 years old and in school, you might want to join the 4-H Dog program to share fun with your dog.

If you want your dog to compete in something fun, he can learn agility at Geyser Creek or at the Rocky Mountain Training Center; he can run, jump and catch at the annual Frisbee competition sponsored by the Jackson/Teton County Parks and Recreation Department, or he can participate in obedience or conformation dog shows. Other annual events include the "Fun Match" at the Teton County Fair sponsored by the Grand Teton Kennel Club, the Dog Show in Driggs during the 4th of July celebration, and the annual Pet Fair co-sponsored by Teton County PAL and PAWS of Jackson Hole to kick off National Pet Week in May.

Some dogs encourage their humans to join the Grand Teton Kennel Club to help promote positive people-dog relationships and learn responsible pet care. Some Teton County dogs do other things that keep them busy. Sled Dogs put in a good day's work. Some Teton County dogs compete in field trials. If the dogs could talk, they would probably say that what they do is fun and not work.

Activities that take much more time and commitment, but that are rewarding for both your dog and yourself, are the Wyoming K-9 Search and Rescue, the Jackson Hole Ski Patrol Avalanche Rescue Dogs and Teton County PAL.

Dog lovers of all degrees are member of PAWS of Jackson Hole, friends of companion animals.

4-H Dogs

by Juanita McGhee

Under the sponsorship of the Teton County Extension Service, 4-H is an important part of many children's lives in Jackson Hole. The Teton County 4-H dog program, which promotes responsible dog care, education and training, has been in existence for a number of years.

The year for the 4-H dog programs starts with a Christmas party. Fun and games are enjoyed by the children and their dogs. Prizes are given for the best costumes, and goodies are awarded to all.

After the holidays, weekly meetings are scheduled. These include visits to such facilities as the animal shelter, veterinary clinics, the feed store, and sled dog kennels. Some meetings feature educational speakers, groomers, and search-and-rescue as well as police dog demonstrations. Videos on the care and training of our canine friends are an important part of some meetings.

Also on the schedule are "Dog Bowls," during which the 4-H'ers answer a series of questions that have been formulated by the state 4-H dog committee. The questions cover many aspects of the dog, such as breeds, care, and history. The format of the "Bowl" is similar to that of a quiz show, with a moderator who reads the questions and each member of the two or more teams answering in turn. This learning experience finishes with a prize given to the team with the most correct answers. The Jackson 4-H Dog Bowl has included the Afton and Riverton 4-H clubs.

The 4-H club is actively involved in the dog sled races held in Jackson in early February (see "Sled Dogs" in this chapter). The 4-H'ers promote interest in the event, help with preparations, and assist the mushers at both the start and finish.

When the spring weather arrives, the young handlers work outside with their dogs. They practice obedience training, conformation and showmanship. Conformation is practiced to help the 4-H members show off their dogs in the best way. It differs from showmanship in that the dogs are judged in conformation, not the handlers. Members work on the best grooming for their dog, how to show the teeth and bite of the dog, and how to hold the tail in the best position for their breed. They learn how to make the dog "pose" (stand straight), and how to gait at the best speed. Conformation takes knowledge and practice.

During this time, the 4-H'ers and their dogs also take their dogs downtown, having them walk through the area to prepare for their part in the Old West Days Parade. For this event, they dress themselves and their dogs in the theme chosen for that year.

4-H members keep record books, working on them during the year. The record books are a written list of all the meetings the members attend and the events they participate in during the year, either with their dog or related to dogs. The 4-H'ers must also enter all the expenses they have incurred during the year for their dog, such as food, equipment, and veterinarian expenses, as well as any profits they earn, for example, from selling any puppies they raise. The record book is quite extensive and includes a summary of goals and what the 4-H'er has learned. A copy of the record book, or a sample, is turned in for judging and credit at the end of the summer.

Another big project for the 4-H youngsters is demonstrations of their knowledge about dogs. This is done in the spring. Participants choose any dog-related subject and are judged according to a set format. Some practice sessions are held beforehand, and the junior leaders help and encourage the participants. The 4-H'ers need not include their dogs as part of the demonstration. A demonstration with a dog could show the proper technique for brushing a dog's teeth and elaborate on the need to do this routinely. Charts illustrating the procedure and its benefits might also be included. An example of a demonstration without a dog might include pictures and charts of a specific breed that explain the good and bad points of the breed, its history, and purposes.

When school is over for the summer, it is time for weekly practices to prepare for the 4-H dog show at the Teton County Fair. This is the summation of the year's work and all members of the 4-H dog club usually participate. All first place winners are then eligible for the State Fair. Teton County 4-H has had numerous entries do well there.

Another important aspect of the club involves visits to the nursing home (St John's Living Center) by the 4-H members with their dogs. During the school year, one or two members go one afternoon each week after school. This is beneficial for both the children and the nursing home residents, as well as good socialization for the dogs. In the summer, a group visits after their weekly outdoor practices.

4-H puts on an informal dog show at the nursing home, where the young people can show some of the things their dogs have been learning. Most of the residents enjoy the interactions with the dogs as well as the company of their young owners.

There are about 15-20 members in Teton County 4-H, age 9 and older. For further information, contact the Teton County Extension office at (307) 733-3087, or your school office. The current adult leders are John Spahr and Juanita McGhee.

Agility Dogs

by Oatsy Von Gontard

Agility is a sport in which a handler is allowed a certain amount of time to direct his or her dog through a series of obstacles while the dog is offleash. The obstacles are arranged in a random course, usually about 180 yards long, in a set sequence. The course snakes around inside an area of about 100 square feet. The goal is to complete the course with the highest score or the quickest time possible. Rules require that the handler cannot touch either the equipment or the dog but can give any number of commands or signals to their dogs. Dogs compete only against dogs of similar height, within a fixed number of jump height divisions. Competitions are held in local, national and international venues and each has its own requirements and regulations.

Certain obstacles are common to all events: pipe tunnel, weave poles, A-frame, dog walk, teeter-totter, collapsed tunnel, pause table, tire or hoop jump, and other types of jumps. The obstacles are designed for dog safety as well as for spectator appeal. It is exciting for spectators to watch a dog and handler in their enthusiastic race against the clock.

Agility trials are open to all dogs but working dogs of medium build tend to be the most successful in agility competitions. However, outstanding individuals of nearly every breed perform well in local and national events. Less agile dogs (usually the larger giant breeds and to some extent the short-legged, long-backed breeds) rarely compete in international events.

Any healthy, fun-loving dog and person can do agility. To clarify, the dogs are the agility experts — jumping small jumps, climbing up and down obstacles, and dashing through tunnels, to name just a few. The people are the cheerleaders — praising, encouraging, laughing and doling out food treats and tactile rewards for canine efforts.

Agility is a "stress-buster." The goal is for your dog and you to have fun while working together as a team in the great outdoors. Agility is a great excuse to spend time with your dog, get some exercise, and enjoy other dogs and dog enthusiasts.

For information on class schedules and play days, call Oatsy Von Gontard at the Rocky Mountain Canine Training Center office at (307) 733-0153. Norina Fields also offers agility at Geyser Creek in Dubois (307-455-2702).

Frisbee Dogs

by Terrie Fair

Here's an exciting event for dogs, dog owners, and spectators. Because Jackson is such a dog-oriented community, the Teton County/Jackson Parks and Recreation Department has recently started to promote the Alpo Canine Frisbee Disc Championship. This national event was originally known as the Ashley Whippet Invitational, founded 23 years ago, by the late, legendary canine Ashley Whippet.

This event is easy, fun, exciting for everyone, and free. The materials are donated by the sponsor and there is no entry fee for the competitors. All contestants receive a Certificate of Achievement, with additional awards going to the winners and runners-up.

This is an athletic competition for dogs. The event is open to all dogs who can catch (or attempt to catch) a frisbee. Border collies usually excel at this event, although awesome aussies, leaping labs, rambunctious retrievers, and magnificent mutts also take to the skies. Points are awarded by the distance of the catch, and whether the dog caught the frisbee in midair, with one paw touching the ground, or with two paws touching the ground. The event consists of two 60-second rounds called mini-distance competition. Competitors receive points for all catches awarded within the allotted time.

What makes this event exciting is that it can be hard to know how you or your dog will perform. Some dogs have caught the frisbee and kept on running. Some dogs do not bother to do anything. And other dogs prefer to visit with the spectators.

However, the frisbee-event veterans do put on a wonderful show. The event in Jackson has been honored by the presence of David Bootes and Chico, demonstrating freestyle before and after the local contestants. David and Chico are winners of the Western Regionals held in California and were contestants at the world championships in Washington DC.

The Alpo Canine Frisbee Disc Championship is held in Jackson on the first Saturday of June. The event takes place in the field between the Recreation Center and Colter Elementary School. Registration is held from 9:00 am to 9:45 am, and the fun starts at 10 am. So, start practicing and get yourself and your dog some exercise.

For more information, contact the Teton County/Jackson Parks and Recreation Department at (307) 733-5056.

Show Dogs

by Juanita McGhee

Your dog can participate in two types of shows: conformation and obedience. However, if you wish to compete with your dog in licensed American Kennel Club (AKC) shows, it is necessary that you travel outside of Jackson Hole. Many locations in Idaho (Idaho Falls, Blackfoot, Pocatello, Boise) as well as other cities in Wyoming (Casper, Laramie and Cheyenne) sponsor AKC events. If you want, you can travel farther to Utah (Ogden or Salt Lake City) and numerous cities in Montana and Colorado.

If you are just starting to show your dog, you will want to consider starting with the events that are called "matches." These do not count toward points but do provide experience. Another feature is that the entry fee is lower. Idaho Falls is the nearest location that holds matches in conformation. The nearest shows with both conformation and obedience are held in Blackfoot Idaho. These four-day events are regularly held in June.

On the local level, the Grand Teton Kennel Club conducts an open show at the Teton County fair each summer. This fun event does not earn points but affords both dogs and owners some good experience. It includes obedience and conformation, puppy sweepstakes, plus a class for mixed breeds, called All American.

Only a few people from Teton County currently compete with their dogs in the dog show game. Any newcomers to the sport are most welcome. Contact Juanita McGhee for further information at (307) 733-2084.

Pet Fair

by Judy F. Eddy

National Pet Week, held during the first week of May, is a time to celebrate the joy of pets. National Pet Week is sponsored by the American Veterinary Medical Association (AVMA), its Auxiliary, the American Animal Health Association, and the North American Veterinary Technician Association.

In Jackson Hole, the Pet Fair was originally sponsored by Teton County PAL. This function is now taken over by PAWS of Jackson Hole. The Pet Fair features ongoing demonstrations throughout the day. Watch search and rescue dogs, hunting dogs, sled dogs, agility dogs, frisbee dogs; ask questions at the informative booths; enter the raffles to win prizes for your dog; and participate in the games and contests for your pets and yourself. This is an event to which your well mannered dog and other pets are especially invited.

Children and their pets can enter the costume contest, as well as have their pet "compete" for prizes including the fluffiest, chubbiest, softest, largest, and other equally intriguing categories. Big Dogs@Petsmart.com is the sponsor of this fun-filled event, and is donating many fabulous prizes.

Teton County PAL distributes information about their programs: Pet Partner® teams and Friends. You can also get a copy of their latest newsletter, and participate in practice evaluations to find out if you and your dog could become a Pet Partner® team.

Teton County veterinarians sponsor a booth where you can ask about any problems your dog might have. Trainers are available to answer questions about obedience and behavior.

The Jackson/Teton County Animal Shelter booth is set up so you can license your dog. Along with the Teton Valley Humane Society, our local animal shelter will have pets available for adoption.

Various pet-related businesses in Teton County have booths, so you can buy or just browse. Groomers, pet sitters, pet photographers, and others also participate. Future plans call for a Canine 9-K run, a dog parade, and events such as an owner-pet look-alike contest, a canine crooning contest, and even an attempt at the world's longest down-stay.

For further information, contact Judy Eddy at (307) 733-9167.

Grand Teton Kennel Club

by Sandy Strout

The Grand Teton Kennel Club is a nonprofit organization located in Jackson. All profits are used to promote humane treatment of dogs. The Club contributes to charities for animals, to special projects initiated by local veterinarians, and to the Jackson Hole Community Pathways to help dog owners dispose of dog poop.

The Grand Teton Kennel Club offers group obedience classes to people who are interested in training their dogs. The fall and spring classes consist of seven sessions each, and owners are supported by much individual help if needed or requested. The puppy classes (for puppies 8 weeks to 14 weeks old) emphasize interactive play, socialization exercises and bonding. The basic obedience classes are for dogs six months and older. Partnership with the owner/handler, and skills that promote a well behaved and happy companion are taught. Advanced classes emphasize learning that will be needed for obedience trials, agility courses, or other dog sports. Problem behaviors can also be worked on.

Obedience classes are free for all dogs who are spayed or neutered within six months of adoption from an animal shelter. Half-price discounts for the classes are offered to all those who adopt a dog from the Jackson/Teton County Animal Shelter if the dogs are not fixed.

In addition to obedience classes, the Kennel Club hosts a "Fun Match" at the Teton County Fair. This show, held on the Saturday during the Fair, is open to all dog owners (adults and young people 12 and older) who want to participate in conformation and obedience events. The show is meant to be educational and fun, and to promote good sportsmanship with dogs. Children in 4-H are also encouraged to participate in the open show. See "Show Dogs" for more information.

The Grand Teton Kennel Club attempts to work in conjunction with the other animal organizations in the County to promote positive owner-dog relationships, good care of animals, and helpfulness wherever it is needed.

Members and volunteers are always welcome. To join the Grand Teton Kennel Club, or for further information, contact
Sandy Strout
855 Ponderosa Drive
Jackson WY 83001
(307) 733-7684

Sled Dogs

by Judy F. Eddy

Sled dogs in Jackson Hole take on special importance in the month of February when international competitors participate in the International Rocky Mountain Stage Stop Sled Dog Race. The Stage Stop is the largest dog sled race in the lower 48 states, and attracts mushers from around the world to compete for substantial financial prizes.

The mushers travel through 14 Wyoming communities in 10 days, starting in downtown Jackson and ending in Teton Village. Teton County 4-H dog club participants promote interest in the event, help with preparations, and assist the mushers at both the start and finish of the race.

The race is run in short stages that average 30 to 80 miles a day. Each day starts a new stage, with the mushers starting in the reverse order of their arrival the previous day. Accumulated times are added and the team with the fastest time wins.

In its first three years, the race became second in popular interest only to the world-famous Iditarod in Alaska. The Iditarod celebrates the transportation of medicine to remote outposts by sled dog teams.

The International Rocky Mountain Stage Stop Sled Dog Race is a qualifying event for the Iditarod. The stage format is easier on the dogs than is a format like that of the Iditarod, in which the mushers cover hundreds of miles over several days between stops. In the local event, the mandatory rest stops allow the mushers and the race veterinarians more chances to examine the dogs, giving those dogs who need it a chance to rest instead of race.

Teton County residents Frank Teasley, an Iditarod competitor, and Jayne Ottman, a former public health nurse, are cofounders of the race. One purpose of the race is to promote awareness throughout Wyoming about childhood vaccinations for preventable diseases.

A second purpose is to make sled dog racing more accessible to the public. As the race stops in various towns each night, the community cheers the teams, provides hospitality to the mushers, and the dogs and mushers expose the community to the experience of sled dog racing.

Another purpose is to promote community development and collaboration between various communities in the state — Wyoming pulling together for partnership, cooperation, and economic viability.

According to Frank Teasley, the race director, some of the finest canine veterinarians in the world monitor the health of the dogs each day at the start, finish, and along the race course. The dogs get EKGs, samples are taken of their blood and urine to ensure proper hydration, and their feet and coats are examined. A computer chip is inserted just under the skin of each dog to track that animal's vital statistics.

To ensure that the dogs are ready for each day's event, the musher can choose from up to 14 of his or her dogs to make up that day's team, helping to ensure that the dogs running that day are at their full strength.

Not everyone can, or wants to, participate in a sled dog race. But for those who want to experience the excitement of mushing, there are several commercial outfits available in Teton County (check the Directory of Dog Services).

The Jackson Hole Retriever Club and Field Trial Dogs

by Ron Kiehn

The Jackson Hole Retriever Club

The Jackson Hole Retriever Club was established in 1985 and operated in the first year as the Bighole Basin Retriever Club. For many years, a field trial was held near Lovell (Wyoming) and the club was named the Bighorn Basic Retriever Club. The membership in and around Lovell lost interest in a retriever club and in the work of sponsoring a field trial. They agreed to help a group in Jackson begin a club and in the following years the club became the Jackson Hole Retriever Club.

Bill and Mary Glenn carried on the work of holding an annual field trial the third weekend of July for many years. Bill and Mary had a wonderful Golden retriever, "Zeke," who distinguished himself by becoming an Amateur Field Champion as recognized by the American Kennel Club.

The present club members intend to expand the organization, to hold training sessions in which members can help each other, to continue the annual field trials and possibly start a hunt test trial. The hunt test trials are a newer innovation licensed by the American Kennel Club. They require dogs and handlers to compete against standards rather than against other dogs and handlers. They also require lesser levels of performance than field trials and are designed to bring more people into the sport.

Field Trials

The first field trials of Labrador retrievers in the United States took place in 1931 and the format was simulated hunting, much different from today's field trials. The format of today's field trial is partially prescribed by the American Kennel Club, but for a dog to meet the requirements leaves a great deal of discretion with the judges. Each dog must be tested on "marks" and "blinds" in both land and water. A mark is a bird that a dog has seen shot and seen where it falls. A blind is a bird that is planted in a location known to the handler but not to the dog. The handler must direct the dog to the bird with hand signals, verbal commands and whistle commands.

The South Park Elk Feedground is the site for the Jackson Hole field trial, and is usually held at the end of July. American Kennel Club field trials have four stakes or Divisions. The first stake is the Open, in which dogs of all ages, handled by professional handlers or amateurs, compete. The second stake is the Amateur in which only amateur handlers can compete. The third stake is the Qualifying in which both professional or amateur handlers can compete but the dog must not have previously placed in an Amateur or Open Stake. The fourth stake is the Derby, in which competing dogs must be less than 2 years old. The Derby is where new people generally start their Field Trial experience.

Jackson Hole Champions

There are two Field Champion Labrador retrievers in Jackson, both owned by the author. One is "Velvet" (full name is Carrols Black Velvet) and the other is "Flip" (full name is Clubmead Head over Heels). Velvet is also an Amateur Field Champion.

For more information on the Jackson Hole Field Trials, or the Jackson Hole Retriever Club, contact

Ron Kiehn at (307) 739-9431; Jolynn Coonce at (307) 733-3730; or Mary Lohuis at (307) 733-2047. All can be reached at the Jackson Hole Retriever Club, Inc. PO Box 4722, Jackson WY 83001.

Search and Rescue Dogs

by Janet Wilts

Wyoming K-9 Search and Rescue (S.A.R.) is a nonprofit organization dedicated to training search dogs and participating in searches. At any given time there are between 5 and 15 members. We are always looking for new handlers and members. Because of our vast wilderness areas and the two national parks, our teams are used frequently.

We take turns having our dogs search for us as we practice being "victims" who need to be found. We all love working with dogs and have found this to be a wonderful way to give back to the community while spending quality time with our dogs. We each train our own dog with the help of other members and other dog groups.

Our group allows us to become certified in as many of the following areas as we choose, although we do not have to certify in all of them:

- Tracking (following a specific person's scent in the wilderness or in town)
- Wilderness search (searching a larger area for a victim)
- Avalanche search
- Water search
- Evidence search (looking for many types of items such as guns, casings, clothes, and keys)
- Cadaver search
- Building search

Our members dedicate much time training our dogs to the highest standard possible. It takes from one to three years to train a dog to the level where he will pass the certification test. Total hours for the first year usually range between 500 and 1500. Once the dog becomes certified, less time is needed to ensure a high level of competency, and to train for other areas of certification. National standards ensure that our dogs are qualified to search anywhere in the country.

Many types of dogs are suited for searching. However, the most easily trained and highest level of success seems to be with dogs in the working class. These dogs include German Shepherds, Golden Retrievers, Labradors, and Border Collies, just to name a few. Many types of dogs can do the work but high-drive dogs of these breeds have more of a chance of passing. Many dogs are not able to get certified due to temperament or other problems.

Wyoming K-9 S.A.R. members are called out by various agencies including the National Park Service, the Forest Service, the Bureau of Indian Affairs, and the sheriff offices in Teton County, Fremont County, Park County, and Sublette County. We also respond to requests from other states, including Idaho and Montana. Some of our searches have been for missing children, hunters, suicide victims, water searches in the Snake River and Flaming Gorge, cadaver searches in Grand Teton National Park and Teton and Sublette Counties, and avalanche victims in Yellowstone National Park and Bridger-Teton National Forest.

Handler skills are just as important as are the dog's skills. Our members receive training in the following areas, depending on their goals:

• Map and compass, orienteering
• Swiftwater rescue
• Skiing (avalanche training, transceiver searchers, probe line assistant)
• First aid
• Climbing, knots and technical rescue
• Survival skills
• Dog behavior and obedience
• Hiking and backpacking skills
• Radio procedures
• Incident command and managing search
• Search skills and techniques
• Clue awareness and securing the scene

If you have any interest in joining us, volunteering as practice victims, or if you have questions, you can contact us by phone or in writing. Because we are a nonprofit group, donations to Wyoming K-9 S.A.R. are tax-deductible. All donations can be made to Wyoming K-9 S.A.R. and mailed to the following address.

Janet Wilts
PO Box 136
Moose WY 83012

You can call Janet Wilts at (307) 734-9052 or Amanda Soliday at (307) 543-2915

Jackson Hole Ski Patrol Avalanche Rescue Dogs

by Jake Elkins

Since 1980, the professional Ski Patrol of the Jackson Hole Mountain Resort has maintained a continuous program that uses avalanche rescue dogs. Over the years, golden retrievers and black and yellow Labradors are contracted by the resort to provide efficient and quick rescue of avalanche victims on the permitted ski area. Additionally, the dogs are used by Teton County, the National Park Service and the National Forest Service in conjunction with other K-9 rescue programs.

Each dog is owned by a professional ski patroller who works for the Jackson Hole Ski Patrol. The dogs are not only highly trained professional rescue dogs, but treasured members of the patroller's family, as well as fellow "workers" on the ski patrol, sharing the patrol stations and demanding their share of "couch time."

Training of the dogs begins when they are very young puppies, and includes basic and advanced obedience, early games of hide and seek, and searching for such articles as backpacks and skier clothing. As the dog's skills develop, basic snow skills are started, with the dog searching first for the handler partially buried, then fully buried, and eventually searching for other volunteers who are fully buried. The dogs are trained to ride on chairlifts and the aerial tramways, ride in a toboggan, stay out of the way of skiers, and maintain their focus during drills. Gradually, the dogs are brought up to the level of competent and dependable avalanche rescue dogs.

Throughout the ski season, the dog handlers continually conduct drills to train and hone the skill of the dogs. Roomy snow caves are dug to house "victims" during the drills, and elaborate scenarios that imitate natural avalanches are devised to provide both dog and handler more experience with slides and buried victims. These drills not only train and maintain the talents of the dogs but also teach the handler how to "read" the dog so they can work as a competent team. Untold hours of training, during both summer and winter, go into the making of a dependable avalanche rescue dog.

In addition to their regular training, many of the dogs travel with their handlers to Alaska and Canada to participate in avalanche dog certification trials. The dogs are used as standby rescuers for extreme skiing events. In other cases, the dogs might spend a winter in an exchange patrol program with ski areas in France. The Jackson Hole dog handlers host an annual rescue scenario for the Teton County Search and Rescue, and have hosted seminars given by the search-dog consultant for the Royal Canadian Mounted Police.

In April 1992, this commitment to hard work was rewarded with the first find of a live avalanche victim in North America, a rescue attributed to "Coup," an avalanche rescue dog on the Jackson Hole Ski Patrol.

For further information, contact Jake Elkins at (307) 733-2292

The canine nose provides the dog with his most powerful sense. While we observe life with our eyes, your dog observes life with his nose. To give an idea of how important a dog's nose is, consider that 1/8 of your dog's brain is dedicated to the sense of smell.

Teton County PAL

by Judy F. Eddy

Pet Partner® Teams

Teton County PAL (People Animal Love) is a nonprofit organization that promotes the human-animal bond by sharing the joy and comfort that an animal can bring. Teton County PAL is affiliated with the national Delta Society, whose mission is to promote mutually beneficial relationships between animals and people to help people improve their health, independence and quality of life. The Delta organization, founded in 1977, has created a powerful network of people who share their belief that contact with animals is important to people's health and well being.

Teton County PAL consists of volunteers and their pets who visit the residents of the local nursing home (St John's Living Center), students at C-Bar-V Ranch, home healthcare patients, hospice patients, the public health nurse clinics, and patients at St John's Hospital. They also work with Community Entry Services (CES) clients. Teton County PAL is in the process of teaming up with the physical therapists in Teton County. Extensive literature provides evidence of a positive therapeutic effect when animals are used as motivators for therapy work.

The PAL volunteers consist of Pet Partner® teams (a human and an animal). People who like people, and sociable animals who like people, make the best Pet Partner® teams. Currently, Teton County Pal has approximately 100 human and animal Pet Partner® teams.

Companion animals have positive effects on the quality of life. Teton County PAL Pet Partner® teams are eager to share the benefits of contact with animals. The social effects of pets include the well known "lubricant" effect. People talk more readily to a person with an animal than to one without. The presence of animals also helps to teach children how to socialize with animals, as well as with other people. Animals help to counteract loneliness, especially for the elderly, for whom a pet might represent the only daily contact that they have with another living thing.

Scientific studies have shown that pet caregivers have stronger heartbeats than do people who do not have pets. Other documented effects include a fall in blood pressure when interacting with an animal. After a heart attack, people who have pets tend to live longer compared with people who do not have pets. Pet owners who have chronic diseases also live longer.

A recent study reported that therapy animals who visited the intensive care unit of the UCLA Medical Center were well received by the patients. Without exception, all the patients who received visits said they would recommend Pet Partner® teams to a friend or relative, and wanted to have the teams visit more frequently.

Currently, Teton County PAL Pet Partner® therapy animals include many dogs, as well as a few cats, a parrot, and a horse. Some of the dog breeds include the Portuguese water dog, the golden retriever, the labrador retriever, the collie, the German shepherd dog, the Weimaraner, and a variety of mixed breeds.

Any group or individual who would benefit from a visit of a Pet Partner® team is encouraged to contact Teton County PAL.

Pet Partner® Team Evaluations

Teton County PAL is always willing to evaluate handlers and animals for qualification and certification as Pet Partner® teams. These evaluations are scheduled approximately every four months. A licensed Delta Society evaluator assesses a team's suitability to volunteer with Teton County PAL. Currently, the fee for an evaluation is $15.

The evaluation consists of a modified Canine Good Citizen test, as well as an aptitude test. These evaluations are not limited to dogs; the obedience portion of the evaluation is slightly different for other types of animals. The aptitude test consists of what a Pet Partner® team might encounter on a visit. Volunteer helpers are in wheelchairs and on crutches, clumsily pet the animal, and cause other distractions. Both members of the team must pass the evaluation. The evaluator must be certain that both the volunteer and the animal interact well with each other, with other people, and with the surroundings. In addition, the human volunteer must pass a written test, the information for which is available in a homestudy course. The homestudy course includes a book and videotape. The Delta Society charges $36 for this course and it is available from Teton County PAL.

The animal must also have a physical examination by a veterinarian. Local veterinarians perform this examination for free. Along with the required paperwork, the volunteer submits a photograph of himself or herself with the animal, plus a registration fee for Delta Society. This fee is currently $35 (less for seniors and youths, and for additional animals with the same volunteer). The Delta Society provides liability insurance and a badge with the photograph for identification as a Pet Partner® team.

When the application is approved by the Delta Society, the Pet Partner® team can visit at St John's Living Center, or any of the other locations in Teton County that are set up for such visits.

Newsletter

Every quarter, Teton County PAL publishes a newsletter for Pet Partner® teams and their friends in the community. This highly acclaimed newsletter contains helpful advice, humor, and information about the Teton County PAL program. For a free copy of the most recent issue, send a self-addressed stamped envelope to Teton County PAL, PO Box 10023, Jackson WY 83002.

Friends

Friends is a special project of Teton County PAL. Friends is made possible by a generous financial donation from Teton County residents Foster and Lynn Friess. The program provides both financial and physical assistance to Teton County residents who need help caring for their pet. Any elderly or disabled person who needs help taking care of a pet either financially (e.g., a security deposit for an apartment) or physically (e.g., the care of a pet when the owner is hospitalized) can apply to the Friends program. Contact Joyce Corcoran at St John's Living Center, (307) 739-7461.

All services provided by Teton County PAL can be confidential. Teton County PAL is a nonprofit organization. Donations comprise its sole source of funding, and all donations are welcome.

For further information, contact
Teton County PAL
PO Box 10023
Jackson WY 83002
(307) 733-9167
tcpal@rmisp.com
http://www.dogsaver.org/tetoncountypal

"In the world which we know, among the different and primitive geniuses that preside over the evolution of the several species, there exists not one, excepting that of the dog, that ever gave a thought to the presence of man."

Maurice Maeterlinck
"Our Friend, the Dog"

PAWS of Jackson Hole

by Judy F. Eddy

PAWS of Jackson Hole is a "friend" of the Animal Shelter, as well as the focus of the community's involvement with companion animals — dogs and cats.

The stated purpose of PAWS of Jackson Hole is the promotion of programs to break the pet overpopulation cycle, fostering of the humane ethic, and prevention of cruelty to, and relief of suffering by, companion animals. These goals are to be achieved through education activities and programs made possible through fundraising efforts throughout Teton County and surrounding areas.

The major goals of PAWS are to
- Reduce the overbreeding of companion animals (specifically dogs and cats) through public education and spay and neuter programs
- Help maintain a vaccination program (rabies) and tag all companion animals in Teton County
- Develop a long-range plan reflective of the animal welfare needs of our area
- Implement a continuous program of fundamental, widespread education to develop humane attitudes toward companion animals, aimed at both children and adults
- Aid the Jackson/Teton County Animal Shelter though fundraising, volunteer support, and resource development
- Help foster the humane movement into regional communities where there is no organized protection for companion animals
- Maintain a good working relationship with veterinarians in the area

PAWS intends to raise awareness among all dog (and cat) owners in our community about responsible pet ownership, while at the same time sponsoring activities and events that the entire community can participate in and enjoy (e.g., a dog park, an expanded Pet Fair, a dog-a-thon, and more). Other projects and activities include establishing a fund for spaying and neutering companion animals for financially needy pet owners and a fund for treatment of injured stray dogs and cats, working with local landlords to encourage them to accept companion animals, finding and supplying shelters for companion animals in case of a natural disaster, and establishing a hot line for the emergency adoptions of companion animals.

All members of the community, not just dog and cat owners, are encouraged to participate in PAWS activities and events. However, these activities and projects will be just that much more exciting for the dog owners in Jackson Hole.

PAWS is a nonprofit organization and as such, is eligible for your tax-deductible contribution. For further information about PAWS, or to make a contribution, please write to PAWS of Jackson Hole, PO Box 13033, Jackson 83002.

Statistics

In 1997 a survey was undertaken by Colorado State University on behalf of the National Council on Pet Population Study and Policy. They received 1996 statistics from 1038 regional shelters and tallied the impoundment of nearly 2,000,000 dogs and 1,500,000 cats. Of these, only about 18% (360,000) of dogs were reclaimed, about 26% (520,000) were adopted, and 56% (1,120,000!!!) were euthanized. Only 25% (375,000) of cats were adopted and 72% (1,080,000!!!) were euthanized. Only 30% of these sheltered and euthanized animals are unadoptable (because they are vicious or ill). The rest are victims of overpopulation and uncaring or unthinking owners.

In this sampling, more than a million dogs and a million cats were euthanized. Nationally, estimates of euthanasia range from 10 to 16 million cats and dogs yearly. A 1998 article in USA Today reported that 85,000 animals are destroyed yearly in Houston — equating to 20 tons of dead pets being taken to the dump every week!!!

This is an abominable situation; every pet should be a wanted animal. Yet, only one in six pets stays with the same family his entire life. The average time someone owns a dog is five years, and the average time for a cat is four years. These animals do not deserve to be a statistic of our throwaway society.

Although Teton County's numbers are remarkably good compared with the above sampling, we cannot afford to relax or consider ourselves immune from overpopulation and euthanasia issues. At the Shelter, animals are regularly abandoned or surrendered by their owners. This is often a result of a change in a living situation, as in renting where pets are not allowed, or returning to school, or even a personal decision to "not be bothered" by pet ownership any longer.

Pet overpopulation is not an imaginary problem. Do your part to help control these numbers and help eliminate the need to euthanize — SPAY and NEUTER YOUR PETS!!!

6 Animal Shelters

Jackson/Teton County Animal Shelter

by Corie Rybak

The Jackson/Teton County Animal Shelter has been in its present facility on Adams Canyon Road since October 1996. The Shelter is a law enforcement entity that also provides a public service. It reports to and is supervised by the Jackson Police Department. It is jointly funded by the Town of Jackson and Teton County. The Town employs three year-round Community Service Officers whose duties include animal control, and the County employs a full-time Animal Control Officer.

The primary function of the Shelter is to provide humane care to the animals who come through its doors (which includes educating their owners). For some impounded animals it is a very brief stay; for surrendered animals, it is hopefully a temporary situation; and for some, it is their final home.

No matter their status, all animals receive the same basic care and consideration. The kennels, water and food bowls are cleaned and sanitized daily. Dogs are housed in individual kennels, indoors during the night and outdoors (under cover) during the day. It is easiest to view the dogs when they are outside where their barking is not as loud.

Cats have their own separate room with private cages, some of which have a "split level" for perching. Their litterboxes are changed daily, as well as their food and water. Each cat has a chance to stretch its legs and explore the shelter when its cage is being cleaned.

Occasional "odd" guests, such as ferrets, rabbits, birds, and so forth, are housed in a cage apart from the dog and cat rooms until more appropriate arrangements can be made.

All animals are fed dry food (the brands vary, depending on donations, which are always welcome), and they are provided with fresh water daily. Canned food is fed as a treat when it is available (again, donations are always welcome).

Animals are observed for signs of injury or illness, and treated appropriately.

Regular operating hours at the Shelter are 9 am to 12 noon, and 1 pm to 5 pm, Monday through Friday. To find the Shelter, drive south out of town on Highway 89 (toward Hoback Junction). Approximately 1-1/2 miles past the High School Road traffic signal, you will see the sign for Adams Canyon Road. After you take that left turn (the Recycling Center will be off to the right), head up the hill to the left. You will see a sign for the Shelter and hear the dogs welcoming you. The phone number for the Shelter is (307) 733-2139.

Impounds

Dogs and cats are impounded at the Shelter, either by law enforcement officers or the general public. These animals are usually found wandering about without their owner, and are brought in for safekeeping. If the animal is wearing a license or other identification, every effort is made to contact his owner as soon as possible.

Before the impounded animal will be released, the owner will have to pay an impound fee (currently $20) and board ($8 a night), and provide proof of rabies vaccination (or be charged for it). The dog will also be licensed if appropriate, and a citation issued if an Officer deems it necessary.

Any impounded animal is held for six days in the hope that his owner will reclaim him. At the end of that holding period, the animal may be put up for adoption.

Surrenders

If people realize that they can no longer keep their pet, for whatever reason (except a history of biting), they can surrender him to the Shelter for a $15 fee. Bringing in the animal's vacci-nation record and providing as much information as possible about the animal will greatly assist in the adoption process, allowing for the most appropriate placement.

The owner should understand that the goal is to find a new home for the animal, but there is the possibility that the animal will eventually be euthanized. There is no set euthanasia sched-ule. It depends on the animal's suitability for placement, health, behavior, number of other animals available, and length of time in the Shelter.

Finding good homes, even for purebred puppies, is diffi-cult. In light of this, concerned owners should make every effort to keep their dog or to find a home for him on their own; surren-dering your dog to the Shelter should be only a last resort.

Adoptions

Animals are always available for adoption at the Shelter. You can read about an available animal in the "Jackson Hole Guide," one of Jackson's weekly newspapers. You can also hear about the animals available for adoption on "Animal Tails," broadcast by Jackson's local radio stations KMTN (96.9 FM) and KSGT (1340 AM) every Wednesday during the noon and 5 o'clock hours. Even if the featured animals are not what you want, come in and check out the others — there are always more.

Animals for adoption are also brought to the Pet Fair that kicks off National Pet Week in May, and Valley Feed's two annual Feed Sales (held on Mother's Day weekend in May and Grandparents' Day weekend in September).

Sometimes, as in the case of surrenders, quite a bit will be known about the animal and his health, habits, and training. Other times, as in the case of strays, guesses will be made as to age, temperament, and training. Unless there is proof to the contrary, it will be assumed that all animals need to have their vaccinations updated.

The adoption fee for dogs is currently $25. Without proof of a current rabies vaccination, the Shelter also requires prepayment for the rabies vaccination ($10) in order to ensure that the owner will take the dog to a veterinarian to get that shot.

Be prepared to visit a veterinarian as soon as possible after adoption of your new pet so that he can be vaccinated against the most common and potentially fatal illnesses he might acquire. Many people who wait too long find themselves with a seriously ill pet and expensive veterinarian bills, made all the more disturbing because the conditions were preventable. The Shelter does not have the means to provide these vaccinations, so be prepared to spend approximately $40 or more for annual preventive veterinary care.

Currently, there is no mandatory sterilization policy because the Shelter is unable to provide the service. However, as an incentive, all the local veterinarians discount their established rate when they spay or neuter animals newly adopted from the Shelter. It is highly recommended that you take advantage of this service. Sending one dog out to a home only to have six unwanted pups come back in later months is not progress, but many steps backward.

The Shelter and its employees make no guarantees about an animal's behavior. Personalities can change when the animal's environment changes. Just removing him from the Shelter and the excitement of the other dogs can bring about amazing transformations; anything is possible. If, however, there are irreconcilable problems within the first week of ownership (especially if there are personality clashes with your existing pets), you can return the animal and your adoption fee will be refunded.

Be patient — life has not been very good to some of these animals, but you have the opportunity to improve it for them.

They are usually very eager to do what is right, and to have someone love them in return.

These animals very rarely come fully trained. Be prepared to spend some time working with your new pet. There are many good obedience trainers in Teton County, not to mention a multitude of training books. Take advantage of the expertise of others. The Grand Teton Kennel Club provides reduced rates to animals adopted from the Shelter at its twice-yearly obedience classes.

Please be sure that you are ready for the responsibility of dog ownership. Have permission to house him in your residence. Many of the animals in the Shelter have been abandoned or surrendered because their owners changed living quarters. Before considering adopting an animal, be sure you are ready for the commitment. Reread Chapter 3 about "Responsibilities of Dog Ownership," and especially, "Alone Again" (page 12) before you decide to adopt a dog.

Licensing

Dogs need to be licensed each January. A license requires proof of current rabies vaccination (good for 2 years in Wyoming).

If the dog resides in Teton County, the current fees are $2 for a fixed animal and $5 for an animal that has not been spayed or neutered. You can get a license at the County Administration Office on Willow Street, as well as at the Animal Shelter.

Town residents pay $5 for a fixed dog and $10 for an intact dog. You can also get a license at the Town Hall on East Pearl Avenue.

Of the approximately 9000 dogs cared for by Teton County veterinarians, only about 10% of them are currently licensed.

Other Services

The Shelter provides other services to the community. Educational materials are available, and group tours can be arranged. The Shelter maintains a Lost and Found record of animals and tries to reunite pets with their owners without impounding the animal. Complaints from the public about problem animals are often directed to the Shelter.

Such equipment as no-bark collars, electronic training collars, and live traps, are available for loan to the public. Be prepared to leave a cost-of-replacement refundable deposit, which varies from $25 to $450, depending on the item you borrow.

The Shelter has quarantine facilities that are used to house animals in isolation from other animals and the public. These facilities are most frequently used after a biting incident to en-sure that the animal is not rabid or carrying any other disease that can be a public health issue.

Local Statistics

In 1998, the average number of dogs housed overnight in the Shelter was 13, with a high of 36 (due to some newborn puppies) and a low of 4. There were an average of 8 cats per night, with a high of 24 and a low of 1. On occasion, one could also find a ferret, rabbit, para-keet or goat.

Every year, approximately 400 dogs are brought into the Shelter. Approximately 70% of these are reclaimed by their owner (after an av-erage stay of one to two days). Approximately 20% of the total number of impounded dogs are adopted (average stay in 1998: 22 days; long-time stay: 143 days). The remaining 10% of the impounded and sur-rendered dogs were euthanized.

Over the years, cat numbers fluctuate greatly as a result of the change in numbers of feral cats trapped for impoundment. Usually, more than 100 cats are brought into the Shelter each year (although there were 200 in 1993). Approximately 60% to 80% of this total are adopted (average stay in 1998: 19 days; longtime stay: 117 days). Per-haps 10% are reclaimed by their owners, while the remainder are euthanized (usually due to poor health or wildness).

Teton Valley Humane Society (Victor and Driggs)

by Tracy Walker

The Teton Valley Humane Society (TVHS) opened its shelter doors in January 1998.

Adoption Service

The TVHS staff works closely with our animals to ensure that they go into homes that match their personalities.

Lost and Found

We maintain a self-service lost and found system during regular shelter hours. Found animals not reunited with their owners during a five-day holding period are accepted at the shelter for possible inclusion in our adoption program. If you have lost an animal, please come by the shelter to review the listings. We also maintain a phone listing of other shelters and impound facilities where your animal might be located.

Education

Education is central to all our services and programs. We strive to inform the public about the humane and ethical treatment of animals through a wide range of formal programs and personal opportunities. We have speakers, films, videos, and literature on a variety of animal welfare and protection issues, such as responsible animal care, companion animal care, over-population, and various public policy positions. We will gladly visit schools, clubs, and organizations, and we provide shelter tours for students and members.

You Can Help

The Teton Valley Humane Society encourages all communities in our area to support our local shelters. There are many ways in which you can help.

Give a little bit. We rely on the support of people like you. Donate treats for dogs or cats, toys, old blankets and towels, or other needed supplies.

Lend a hand. Volunteer your time. Bathe and groom the animals, walk the dogs, or play with the cats.

Find that special someone. Choose your next pet from your shelter. We have wonderful dogs and cats of different sizes, shapes and colors who are just waiting for a permanent, loving home.

Help spread the word. Tell your friends. Promote animal safety and responsible pet ownership.

Be a responsible pet owner. Keep current identification on your dog or cat. Spay or neuter your pets. Give them lots of love and attention.

Tails on Trails

The "Tails on Trails" program provides the opportunity for locals and visitors to take a dog on a hike. Whether you are passing through and just miss your four-legged buddy (who had to stay home) or you live in the area and cannot have a dog, this would give our dogs a chance to go out and give you a chance to get some exercise and have a buddy for a day.

Information

The Teton Valley Humane Society is located at 185 East 25 North, Driggs Idaho 83422. We are open from 10:00 am to 4:00 pm Tuesday through Saturday. We are available before and after hours or on Sundays and Mondays by appointment. Call us at (208) 354-3499, email humanesociety@pdt.net, or see our website at http://www.pdt.net/tvhs

Lots of licks and paws from all of our furry friends.

"If you can't decide between a Shepherd, a Setter or a Poodle, get them all ... adopt a mutt!"   *ASPCA*

Because your dog's eye is flattened, it is more sensitive to light and movement but is less able to resolve close vision. Your dog is farsighted — he cannot see well "right under his nose."

7 Natural Disasters
by Judy F. Eddy

Teton County is vulnerable to earthquakes, forest fires, landslides, dam failure and flooding. Are you prepared to take care of your dog in case of such a natural disaster?

Different disasters require different responses. In some cases, you might have to evacuate your home. If you must evacuate, the most important thing you can do to protect your dog is to evacuate him, also. Leaving him behind, even if you try to create a safe place for him, is likely to result in his being injured, lost, or worse.

Under stress, which you will also most probably be feeling if you have to evacuate, your dog might react differently from usual. Outside your home and in the car, keep him securely leashed. Don't leave him unattended where he can run off. When panicked, the most trustworthy dog might hide, try to escape, or even bite.

Teton County Disaster Services are affiliated with the American Red Cross. Red Cross shelters do not allow pets.

Thus, it is up to you to ensure that you have the supplies needed for your dog, at least until (and if) our disaster is serviced by volunteers from E.A.R.S. (Emergency Animal Rescue Service). This nonprofit group, part of United Animal Nation, was founded in California to rescue animals from floods, wildfires, earthquakes and other natural disasters. They set up shelters, and stay as long as needed. You can contact them for more information, to send a donation, or to find out how to be an E.A.R.S. volunteer.

United Animal Nation
E.A.R.S.
PO Box 188890
Sacramento California 95818
916-429-2457

Plan Ahead

NOW is the time to stock up on the items that you will need so you will not get caught unprepared. Do not put off doing what you should do now — it might keep your dog alive if a disaster strikes. At the same time you are preparing your dog's supplies in the event of a natural disaster, you will probably want to update your own emergency kit and supplies.

- collar with identification
- current photo of your dog
- first-aid book and emergency kit
- record of vaccinations
- 2-week supply of food and bottled water

Identification (Collar and Tag)

During a disaster an animal can escape. A collar and tag increase the chances of your pet being returned to you. Remember that phones might not be working, so be sure to include a physical address in addition to a phone number.

Keep an extra collar and identification tag with your disaster supplies in case his permanent one gets lost during a disaster. A spare identification tag with your disaster supplies is useful if you are going to be living somewhere temporarily. Put the phone number and address of the temporary location on the tag. Teton County PAL (307-733-9167) sells inexpensive, easy-to-make identification tags on which you can put your temporary information.

If your dog rides in the car, always have a leash in the vehicle. If a disaster occurs while you are driving and if you should have to leave your car, you want to be able to keep your dog safely controlled.

Consider keeping a dog harness and a 6-foot-long leash with your disaster supplies. A frightened dog can slip out of a collar but not out of a harness.

Photos

Have some current color photographs of your dog in case he gets lost during a disaster (or any other time). Include photographs that show any distinguishing marks that would make it easier to assist in identifying your dog. In case you have to show proof of ownership, include yourself in some of the photographs with your pet. To protect them from possible water damage, store the photographs in a resealable plastic bag. This bag is also a good place in which to keep a copy of your dog's rabies vaccination certificate.

First-Aid Kit

Assembled kits and books can be bought from some pet supply catalogs, or you can make up one yourself. These kits are also invaluable when you are hiking with your dog. Some suggested items include:

- first-aid book for dogs
- conforming bandage (3"x5")

- absorbent gauze pads (4"x4") and absorbent gauze roll (3"x1 yard)
- cotton tipped applicators (1 small box)
- antiseptic wipes (1 package)
- emollient cream (1 container)
- anticoagulant powder
- hydrogen peroxide solution (3%)
- syrup of ipecac
- antibiotic ointment (e.g., neosporin)
- oral syringe
- tweezers and scissors
- needlenose pliers
- instant cold pack
- latex disposable gloves (several pairs)
- proper fitting muzzle

Medications
If your dog is on long-term medication, have available at least a two-week supply because your veterinarian might not be able to fill a prescription. If the medication needs to be refrigerated, you can usually get ice from a Red Cross shelter and put the medicine into an ice chest.

Food
Feeding your dog on his regular routine, the best you can, helps minimize any stress he might be feeling. Always have a reserve supply of the type of food your dog is used to eating that would last at least one week, preferably two. If your dog eats canned food, buy cans small enough to be used at one feeding since you might not have a way to properly refrigerate leftover food. You can use poptop cans or you can include a can opener with your disaster supplies. Do not use canned food that has been opened and not refrigerated for more than a few hours.

Store dry food in an airtight, waterproof container and rotate food at least once very three months. Include with your disaster supplies an extra feeding dish and a spoon to scoop and mix the food.

Water
Although your dog might drink routinely from mudpuddles and even the toilet, conditions can be different during a disaster (e.g., during the 1999 floods in North Carolina, water was contaminated with hog sludge as well as dead animals).

Have enough drinking water to last at least one week, preferably two, for each dog in your household. Store water in a cool, dark location, and be sure to rotate it so it remains fresh. Remember that if the tap water is not suitable for humans to drink, it is also not suitable for animals to drink. Do not let your dog drink flood water or any other water sources that might be contaminated as a result of the disaster. If officials have issued a "boil water" warning, that means that the water is unhealthy for your dog also. If you are drinking bottled water or purified water during a disaster, that is what your dog should be drinking, too.

Include with your disaster supplies an extra water dish, just in case the one normally used is lost.

Treats and Toys

Your dog might be stressed by the commotion and strange surroundings. Any special treats and a favorite toy will help distract and reassure him.

Sanitation

A pooper scooper or plastic bags (Mutt Mitts) should be in your supplies.

Cleaning Supplies

Include with your disaster supplies a small container of liquid soap for washing your dog's food dish. Also include some paper towels for drying dishes and for other cleanup. If you will be housing your dog in a crate, include a disinfectant that can be used to clean the crate.

Temporarily Confining Your Dog

Fences and walls can be damaged or destroyed, making it easier for your dog to escape and get lost. You might wish to buy a plastic airline crate or a wire collapsible crate to transport your dog if you have to evacuate, or to keep your dog contained following a disaster. The crate should be large enough so he can lie down comfortably and still have room for food and water dishes.

A metal tie-out stake that screws into the ground provides a place to fasten a dog chain (not a leash that he can chew through). Be sure the chain is long enough for your dog to move around but not so long that he can get tangled around something. Be sure the stake is secure for your dog's size.

Be sure that your dog is not chained where he could fall off and hang himself (for example, from a porch), and that he will not be exposed to falling tree limbs, shingles, power lines, chimney bricks, or other debris. If you must temporarily stake your dog outside, provide a shelter from the hot sun, extreme cold, snow, rain, or floodwaters. It is also important to stake him where he will be safe from potentially aggressive animals.

Where to Take Your Dog

Red Cross evacuation shelters will not allow animals except seeing-eye dogs and other recognized service dogs. If you are not sure where to take your dog when you evacuate, do not leave him behind because this greatly increases the chances that he will not survive.

Identify ahead of time several possible places where you can take your dog should you have to evacuate. Ideally, these locations would not likely be affected by the same disaster that would hit where you live. These include boarding kennels, veterinary clinics with boarding space, grooming facilities, dog clubs, and training clubs. Do not forget to consider friends and family members, too, for caring for your dog.

For example, if your home might be threatened by flooding, identify safer places at higher elevations. Evacuate before roads are closed, even if you do not know where you can take your dog.

You can use this book to find hotels and motels that accept dogs (see the Directory of Dog Services, Chapter 13). Some lodging that might not normally allow animals might make an exception during a disaster, so it is worth inquiring.

You might want to keep a copy of your dog's medical records with your disaster supplies, but it is more important that you have a record of his rabies vaccination.

Start a buddy system with someone in your neighborhood so that they will check on your dog during a disaster in case you are not home. Agree to do the same thing for them. Exchange information on veterinarians and have a permission slip put in your file at the veterinarian that authorizes your pet to get necessary emergency treatment should you not be reachable.

Jackson/Teton County Animal Shelter

The animal shelter is located at 3150 Adams Canyon Road, south of town off Highway 89 (see specific directions in Chapter 6). Know where it is. You might need to visit it after a disaster to look for your missing dog. It is important to start looking for your pet as soon as you realize he is gone because the shelter might not be able to house large numbers of displaced animals that arrive during a disaster.

Lots of Comfort for Your Dog

Remember that your dog might be frightened — having you nearby will help. Chew toys can help entertain a dog that might have to be chained or confined in a crate for long periods of time. Your dog can also be great comfort to you — soothing him can help soothe your own discomfort.

Fire in Your Home

If your home catches on fire, and you are not there, will the fire department know to look for your dog or other pets? You can alert them to the presence of animals in your home with stickers that you place on your door and/or windows. These are available from Teton County PAL for a nominal cost, and might mean the difference between life and death for your pet. Call (307) 733-9167 to buy your stickers today.

THE TEN COMMANDMENTS
(pet version)

1. My life is likely to last 10 to 15 years. Any separation from you will be painful for me. Remember that before you acquire me.
2. Give me time to understand what you want of me.
3. Place your trust in me — it is crucial to my well being.
4. Don't be angry at me for long and don't lock me up as punishment. You have your work, your entertainment and your friends. I have only you.
5. Talk to me sometimes. Even if I don't understand your words, I understand your voice when you're speaking to me.
6. Remember that however you treat me, I'll never forget it.
7. Remember before you hit me that I have teeth that could easily crush the bones of your hand but that I choose not to bite you.
8. Before you scold me for being uncooperative, obstinate or lazy, ask yourself if something might be bothering me. Perhaps I am not getting the right food, or I've been out in the sun too long, or my heart is getting old and weak.
9. Take care of me when I get old; you, too, will grow old.
10. Go with me on difficult journeys. Never say, "I can't bear to watch it," or "Let it happen in my absence." Everything is easier for me if you are there. Remember, I love you.

8 If Your Dog Gets Lost in Jackson Hole
by Corie Rybak

This chapter is for Jackson Hole residents and the visitors to the valley.

Many people travel with their pets. Traveling with your dog is easier if you plan ahead. A list follows of items that you should have with you, for your and your dog's traveling comfort and enjoyment. All items can be purchased at local suppliers.

- food and water bowls
- can opener
- treats
- favorite toy
- blanket
- old towels
- brush or comb
- scooper and plastic bags (or disposable pooper scooper)
- tweezers, scissors, needlenose pliers (for porcupine quills)
- travel identification with destination numbers (physical address and phone number) or phone number of a friend or relative at home who can reach you. Contact Teton County PAL for an instant, inexpensive 5-minute tag (307-733-9167).
- vaccination certificate and license from your hometown
- leash or harness
- dog photo, in case he gets lost (preferably with you in the photo)

However, that joyful experience of having the entire family on vacation together can be marred in one single second. Within that second, the family dog can embark on a delightful adventure and, in never-before-visited territory, can suddenly become lost.

You will need to take certain precautions to avoid losing your pet in a strange environment. Keeping your dog on a leash is a wise practice, almost guaranteeing that you will remain together. However, there are many places where you will be tempted to let your dog run free. Please do this only if your dog is easily controlled and you are confident that your pet will not run far off if frightened.

Examples of dogs who ran off include a dog on Snow King who was startled by the fireworks on the 4th of July, and was not found until the next day at Goodwin Lake many miles away (we are still trying to figure out what route he took). A dog last seen in Driggs Idaho was found north of Jackson — something scared him, he jumped into the back of someone's pickup truck, and wound up miles from home.

This kind of separation is emotionally tough on both you and your dog, and the best bet is to do everything you can to avoid its occurrence.

If, despite proper precautions, you and your dog do somehow part ways, a few phone calls might help you become quickly reunited. However, before placing those calls, make a reasonable effort to find your critter on your own — thoroughly check your vehicle, motel room, motel lobby, courtyard, and any restaurant where you ate. Sometimes your dog is only looking for something familiar, and might not have strayed too far.

If your brief but intense search fails, find a telephone, make yourself comfortable and start dialing the resources listed below.

When you call, please be prepared to describe your pet: breed, color, sex, collar and tags (if any). Tell where and when you last saw him, and leave your name and phone numbers for future contact.

Jackson/Teton County Animal Shelter
3150 Adams Canyon Road
(307) 733-2139

If your pet is picked up by either law enforcement or a concerned citizen, he will more than likely be brought to the Shelter for safekeeping. The Shelter is open between 9 am and 5 pm, Monday through Friday, and you can call during those hours to learn if your dog is there. At other times, you can leave a message or call Teton County Dispatch (see below).

The Shelter also keeps track of lost and found pets that are not brought in — you can leave information about your animal and how you can be reached, and if someone calls in reporting that they found your pet, the Shelter will assist in bringing the two of you together.

If an animal is cared for at the Shelter, there are associated fees. Pursuant to ordinances, to release any impounded animal currently costs $20, and after the first night there is an $8 per night charge for board. Cash and checks are accepted; no credit card service is currently available.

Teton County Dispatch
(307) 733-2331

Dispatch keeps a list of lost and found pets, and might be able to let you know the status of your animal. He might have been picked up and impounded by Animal Control or law enforcement when no one was at the Shelter to answer your call. You will probably have to wait until the Shelter is open to retrieve your animal, but at least you might be able to find out where he is. Play it safe and leave a similar message on the machine at the Animal Shelter, covering all bases and eliminating the possibility of any oversight.

Veterinarians

Call the local veterinarians. In some cases, someone who finds a dog will bring it to the nearest veterinarian who might keep it for a day or so before giving it to the Animal Shelter. The veterinarians and their telephone numbers are listed in the Directory of Dog Services.

Call Home

If your pet was wearing any identification, such as your home phone, or a rabies tag with your veterinarian's phone number, please call home! If someone found the animal, they might have left a message at one of those numbers.

Grand Teton National Park Dispatch
(307) 739-3301

If your pet escapes while you are touring in the Tetons, the Park might be able to assist you with their lost and found services.

Radio Stations

Jackson Hole's local radio stations will announce lost and found pets as a public service.
KMTN: (307) 733-4500
KSGT: (307) 733-2120
KZ95: (307) 733-1770

Because each of the listed organizations is independently run, it is well worth calling all of them. Also, when you do get your pet back, please be considerate and make some return phone calls so that your name can be taken off of their (often considerably long) lists.

If you observe your dog, you will notice that he can swivel his ears. Unlike human ears, your dog's ears are relatively mobile.

Tribute to a Dog

The one absolutely unselfish friend that man can have in this selfish world, the one that never deserts him, the one that never proves ungrateful or treacherous, is his dog. A man's dog stands by him in prosperity and in poverty, in health and in sickness. He will sleep on the cold ground, where the wintry winds blow and the snow drives fiercely, if only he may be near his master's side. He will kiss the hand that has no food to offer; he will lick the wounds and sores that come in encounters with the roughness of the world. He guards the sleep of his pauper master as if he were a prince. When all other friends desert, he remains. When riches take wing and reputation falls to pieces, he is as constant in his love as the sun in its journey through the heavens.

Senator George Vest, 1870

9 Hiking with Your Dog

by Judy F. Eddy

Sharing Good Times With Your Dog

Many people enjoy taking their dog with them when they hike, bicycle, run, skate or cross-country ski. Exercising with your dog is pleasurable for both of you. You get protection and company, and your dog loves the exercise. Do stop and let him smell occasionally. You might observe the world with your eyes, but your dog does so with his nose.

Be a responsible pet owner. If you exercise with your dog, maintain a pace that is comfortable for him. Your dog ages faster than you do. So, although your dog might be only 5 in dog years, he could already be a 35-year-old in human years. Perhaps you might not slow down much at that age, but your dog might proceed at a much slower pace if allowed to do so. As with people, you should start his exercise with short distances and work up to longer ones over a period of weeks.

Your dog has physical limitations that are different from yours. Never assume he is fine just because he is keeping up with you. Because your dog will not complain, he will not tell you he is in pain.

Responsibilities

When hiking with your dog, you need to exercise common sense. The rule of the trail is: bicycles yield to hikers and horses, and hikers yield to horses. This means that horses always have the right of way, and you and your dog have the right of way over bicyclists. However, a bicyclist coming downhill might have difficulty stopping safely and yielding to you. You can show consideration by controlling your dog and stepping aside to allow the bicyclist to safely pass. If your dog does not have experience with horses, have a leash ready as soon as you see a horse ahead of you on the trail or hear one coming from behind.

When you take your dog for a hike, remember "the three Ls: lunch, liquids, leash." A first-aid kit for dogs is something else you will want with you. You might want to consider having your dog use a dog backpack to carry his own supplies if you take a longer hike than those listed in this book.

Potential Hazards

When you hike with your dog, there are many hazards for you to be aware of. This is not to be alarmist, because the possibility of encountering most of them is slim. Rather it is to let you know about them — forewarned is forearmed.

Running Away

If your dog is not used to walking off leash, realize that when you are hiking with him, he will be tempted to explore every scent and motion he encounters. If he is not under your control, you might end up losing him. Keep him on a leash until he can handle all the scents, sights, and sounds that the outdoors provides. Make sure your dog has an identification tag.

Altitude

Altitude can affect both your dog and you; however, none of the hikes described in this book is high enough in elevation that you might be threatened by serious altitude sickness.

If you are visiting the area or are new to the valley, it might take a while to get used to the higher elevation. If you experience dizziness or a headache, take time to acclimatize and choose a hike with a lower elevation gain. The valley floor is approximately 6200 feet above sea level. Other than the Jackson Hole Community Pathways , the walk on the Snake River levee, and the Elk Refuge, the other hikes do gain altitude. Take it easy at first and remember that your dog might feel the altitude also. One way to avoid problems is to drink plenty of water. If you start to feel ill, walk back down to a lower elevation.

Weather

Weather can change dramatically and suddenly in the mountains, so stay alert to the forecasts. Always be prepared for a snowstorm, thunder and lightning, or hail, no matter what the season. Even at the lower elevation of the valley floor, the weather is variable and unpredictable. It can be sunny in one place and hailing in another, even in the summer. In general, the higher the altitude, the more likely it is to be cold and windy, and the more likely it is to rain or hail.

Summer temperatures in Teton County can range from the 50°s to 80°s and even 90°s, with snow possible even in July and August. If you hike on hot summer days, avoiding the middle of the day will help you and your dog from getting too hot. You will probably want to take him to the Snake River or to a lake where he can take advantage of the cool water. Read the hike descriptions to find one that is sheltered by trees rather than one that is open with no shade. To prevent dehydration, be sure to have plenty of water available for yourself and your dog.

Watch your dog carefully when you run, especially on warm days. Heavy panting and thickened saliva are signals to slow to a walk. Dehydration can be serious. Light-skinned dogs can get sunburn and pink-nosed dogs have been known to get skin cancer on their noses. Use a nontoxic sunscreen for such dogs if you must hike in the sun.

Even though your dog has a fur coat, he can die from winter conditions such as hypothermia or frostbite. Be alert for shivering, cold extremities (legs, paws, ears and tail), lethargy, confusion, or other signs of distress. Contact your veterinarian immediately because untreated hypothermia can lead to death. Frostbitten skin is red or gray and may slough. Contact your veterinarian if your dog exhibits any signs of frostbite.

In the winter, take special precautions when you hike near ponds, streams and lakes. Every year, pets accidentally drown in partially frozen water. When you are on the levee, do not let your dog go onto the frozen ponds unless you are sure he cannot break through the ice and fall in.

Your dog does not wear shoes, so be considerate of his feet. Snow and ice in the winter cause problems for some dogs, forming iceballs in between his toes or cuts from frozen snow. Gravel and hot pavement are unpleasant for some dogs to run on in the summer. Check your dog's feet after a long workout. Some dogs are tenderfooted. To protect his feet, consider some dog booties made of leather or a synthetic fabric. Dogs run more comfortably on soft surfaces, not asphalt.

Snow

Many people take their dogs in the backcountry. During the winter, observe skier etiquette and do not let your dog make tracks where people will be skiing. Taking a dog into the backcountry is not always appropriate, however, because he can start an avalanche. Deep snow can also drain his energy reserves. He will give his all to keep up with you, and his heart and joints might not tolerate the stress.

Horses

If you do enough hiking in Teton County, you will undoubtedly encounter horses on the trails. Not all dogs interact well with horses. Accidents can happen quickly. Be alert to the situation and keep your dog under control. You definitely do not want to be responsible for a mishap. Here are a few hints that are helpful even when you do not have your dog with you.

Horses hate to be surprised. Some horses spook easily and might throw their rider. If a rider asks you to talk to his horse, do so. A few words from you might reassure the horse that no harm will come to it.

When you pass a horse on a trail (the horse has the right of way), say hello and ask the rider what he or she would like you to do to allow a safe passage. This applies to narrow trails as well as to wider fire roads. Generally, the rider will try to find a place safe for everyone, then either ask that you stand still while the horse passes, or move aside and wait until you pass. It is foolish to challenge a thousand-pound animal.

When you share the trail with horses, their droppings will be on the trail. Some dogs will ignore them but others will rapidly gobble up any they encounter, especially if they are fresh. Although disgusting, it is not harmful. If the thought of your dog eating horse manure bothers you, let him get what he can while you make your attempt to stop him. Some dogs enjoy rolling in the manure, which you will probably find objectionable. You can use a leash and reinforce the "leave it" command.

Wildlife

As you hike, you might encounter *moose*, *bear*, *wolves*, *mountain lions*, and other wildlife. You might see a herd of *elk*, a few *deer*, even *coyote* and *red fox*. Your dog will probably detect both *tree squirrels* and *ground squirrels* that you might never see. You will definitely see birds — perhaps the majestic *bald eagle* and *trumpeter swans* soaring in the sky, the *goldeneyes* and *mallards* swimming in the Snake River, or the *water ouzel* dipping in a nearby stream.

Enjoy the animals from a distance, respect their needs to be unmolested, and do NOT let your dog harass any of them. Law enforcement can shoot him if he chases big game.

As a safety precaution, have pepper spray (at least a 9-ounce can) with you when you hike. Oil-based pepper spray is specifically manufactured as a bear deterrent and the EPA registers it for its effectiveness. (See the Directory of Dog Services for suppliers.) The cost ranges from about $30 to $60, and you should replace it every two years. However, this is a small expense when you consider that it will deter bear and moose, and can save your and your dog's lives. Do not hike with your spray "safely" stored in your fanny pack. You want it accessible within seconds.

Bear spray is not 100% effective but it has demonstrated the most success compared with all other means (including firearms) in fending off threatening and attacking bears and preventing injury to the person and involved animal.

When you are hiking with your dog, he can be either beneficial or harmful to you. If he is under control, and stays near you, neither of you should be harmed by wildlife. You do not want to let him run so far ahead of you that he is not under your control.

If you are hiking in *bear* country, know how to act. Be BEar AwarE. Know the signs of bear: scat, tracks, diggings, turned-up logs and turned-over rocks, carcasses, fish remains, broken or bruised fruit shrubs, daybeds, and hairs on trees, rocks or other surfaces. Stay on the trail, and keep your dog close.

If you see a bear, always look for cubs. A sow will be aggressive in her attempt to protect them. Hiking with a dog in bear country can be beneficial if your dog is under control. He will probably sense the presence of a bear long before you do. Stay alert to his actions. However, if your dog is not under control, you should leash him when you are in bear country. If he runs ahead of you and encounters a bear, he will most likely come running back to you and the bear could be right behind him.

Do not hike alone with your dog, or after dark. Make noise — talk, sing, use bells. Use caution where your vision is obstructed. Avoid a bear if you see one; do not approach it. Avoid carcasses; do not let your dog investigate any, either.

If you do encounter a bear, it is important to know how to react based on the motivation for the bear's behavior. If you do have an encounter, the bear will most likely be displaying defensive behavior (surprise encounters, defense of young, and food guarding). Displays might include vocalizations (huffing, growling, popping jaws), staring with head lowered and ears pinned back on its head, body posturing, or bluff charges.

Stay calm — do not panic and do not run. You definitely want your dog under your control at this time. Get your pepper spray ready for use. Slowly detour or back away. Do not block the bear's escape route. Avoid direct eye contact but keep your eyes on the bear. Speak in a soft monotone. Turn sideways so that the bear can see that you are not challenging it, but do not turn your back to it.

If the bear charges, stand your ground. Use your pepper spray and aim directly into its face. Aim low rather than high; the spray will drift up and the bear will be charging low.

If the bear does attack you, play dead. Drop to the ground and curl into a ball, clasping your hands over the back of your neck.

Mountain lions are generally shy and should not be a threat. Although they are most active from dusk to dawn, they do travel and hunt in daylight. Again, stay alert to signs: tracks and scat. In mountain lion territory, do not walk your dog after dark for your own safety and out of respect to the mountain lions. Mountain lions have been seen on the Elk Refuge, Cache Creek, Snow King, Game Creek, and Leeks Canyon.

However, if you should encounter one, do not approach it and keep your dog under control. Stay calm; talk calmly but firmly. Do not run but slowly back away. Your actions in a mountain lion confrontation should be different from those when you meet a bear. You want to appear large — stand tall, wave your arms, open your jacket wide. If with others, stand together. Throw sticks and rocks at it. Do not mimic the behavior of its prey by running away.

If you are attacked, do *not* play dead but *do* fight back, using your fists and whatever else you can. This is another extremely important time to have your dog under your control.

Although *deer* will run from your dog and not turn to chase him, *moose* can and do. They have even been known to attack and kill dogs without provocation. It is best to give them plenty of room — do not try to stare one down if it is upset at your presence. In the winter, there are usually a few moose on the Snake River Levee as well as other locations throughout the County. It is not uncommon for them to completely block your way. Turn around and go elsewhere.

You are more likely to be attacked by a mountain lion or bear than by any other wildlife, and because moose are so unpredictable, they are rather high on the list also.

Wolves are shy of humans so if you are hiking where there might be wolves, keep your dog with you — don't let him wander off!

Coyotes have been known to try to lure dogs to one that is making noises; the pack then will attack the dog.

Some dogs learn from one encounter with a *porcupine* while others never learn, If you have needlenose pliers in your first-aid kit while you are hiking, you might be able to remove the few quills that your dog gets in a "mild" encounter. However, neither would have helped when my black lab "BJ" tried to eat a porcupine. That required an emergency trip to the veterinarian and removal of the quills from his eyes, inside his mouth, his nose, his ears, and all over the rest of his head under anesthesia. If you see a porcupine, it is the right time for your dog to "come" and "leave it" on command, two important obedience commands your dog should respond to automatically.

Badgers are nocturnal and will usually not be seen while you are hiking. But their holes are enticing for dogs to sniff and perhaps start digging. Depending on where you are hiking, their holes are usually off the trail. For the sake of the badger or any other creature living in a hole, and for the terrain itself, do not let your dog dig while you are hiking on public land.

Although *skunk* encounters with a dog are relatively rare, if your dog gets sprayed by a skunk, first rinse his eyes with plain warm water. If your first-aid kit includes a deodorant spray, you can spray it on him right away.

When you get home you can use the following solution to help get rid of the odor. Pour 1 quart of 3% hydrogen peroxide mixed with 1/4 cup of baking soda and 1 teaspoon of liquid soap all over your dog, being careful to keep it out of his eyes. Lather it in and let it sit for a few minutes. Rinse him with lukewarm water and repeat as needed.

Some pet groomers recommend using Massengill, a medicated douche. For a small dog, mix two ounces with one gallon of water. For large dogs, double the amount of water and Massengill. Pour it all over your dog (avoiding his eyes) until it soaks into his fur. Rinse him after 15 minutes and then wash him with his regular shampoo and rinse thoroughly. Scope (the mouthwash) straight from the bottle, followed by thorough rinsing, is also recommended.

Poisonous *snakes* do not live in Teton County so you will not have to concern yourself if you see your dog sniffing at a snake. It is probably a garter snake, which is perfectly harmless (although they do emit a noxious odor in self-defense). Nonetheless, follow the general rule of dogs and wildlife and do not let your dog bother a snake.

Prevention is the best medicine. When you are hiking with your dog, be alert to wildlife before your dog encounters them.

Crucial big game winter ranges throughout Jackson Hole are closed to all human occupancy to protect the wintering wildlife. Because the presence of humans and dogs can stress wildlife, cause them to run, or prevent them from accessing the crucial habitat they need to conserve precious energy and survive the winter, you and your dog are prohibited from entering these areas. The Forest Service posts these locations and it is your responsibility to know them. These areas are not included in the trails designated as friendly for your dog in the winter.

Water

Because your dog drinks from the flowing streams, the river, the ponds and lakes, and even the mud puddles, he is at risk of ingesting giardia. Giardia are protozoans that are encased in cysts. If your dog swallows any, his stomach acid will open the cysts and the giardia can then attach to the wall of his small intestine. Symptoms of giardia can appear one to two weeks later. Diarrhea is the most common symptom but others include loss of appetite, abdominal cramps, and bloating. If not treated, giardia can persist indefinitely, causing weight loss and nutrient deficiencies. Giardia must be diagnosed by a veterinarian, who will probably prescribe either of the antibiotics Flagyl (metronidazole) or Atabrine (quiniacrine). Both medications can cause vomiting and diarrhea (the cure is sometimes worse than the disease), but they are 90% effective.

The potential for ingestion of a giardia cyst during backcountry excursions is something that must be considered by all dog owners. When you take your dog on any of the listed hikes, the availability of water is noted. Stopping your dog from drinking water out of a stream or lake when he is hot or tired from a long hike might be more than you want to attempt. Most people do let their dogs drink freely from the local water.

If you are concerned about the possibility of his contracting giardia, you might want to consider taking fresh water along for him. An easier solution, however, is to get your dog vaccinated with the new giardia vaccine for dogs. Check with your veterinarian; they are recommending it to protect your dog, especially if he is susceptible to giardia infections.

Insects

Fleas and heartworm do not occur in Teton County, but in the springtime your dog might get a tick on him. Always check yourself and your dog when you get home during this time of the year. Don't forget to check his ears and between his toes. If you see one, just pull it straight out with tweezers. If you have removed a tick from your dog and he then gets lethargic for a few days, has a fever, loses his appetite, or becomes lame, have your veterinarian check him. Although dogs traveling into Teton County might be carrying Lyme disease or Rocky Mountain Spotted Fever, these are not endemic to our area.

Foxtails and Burrs

Foxtails are the arrow-shaped seeds of dry grass. They are annoying, and in rare cases can be lethal. Foxtails can stick in your dog's ears, eyes, nose, between his toes, or in his mouth, and then work their way in. Check every nook and cranny of your dog after a walk if you have been near dry grass.

Many of the lovely summer wildflowers become nuisances in the late summer and autumn when the flowers give way to burrs. These burrs stick to most dogs' fur and are a nuisance to remove. Some are extremely tiny while others are the size of acorns! Some dogs get them stuck on their faces and on their eye hairs or in their ears. After and even during a hike, note that your dog might need help in removing burrs. Many dogs will remove those that they can reach, enjoying the grooming aspect of pulling them out. However, your dog will rely on you to remove those he cannot reach.

Other Hazards

Some dogs do not know what an *automobile* can do to them, so be alert at all times. Be especially alert in parking lots where he would be most likely to encounter moving automobiles. Most *snowmobilers* in Teton County are aware of people and dogs using the trails and do slow down.

Skiers and *snowboarders* go fast and are numerous on the Old Pass Road in the winter — be careful. You will most likely meet *bicyclists* on the Old Pass Road or Cache Creek, some of whom go downhill quite rapidly. A bicycle might spook your dog. You do not want him to run in front of a bicycle. Stay alert so you know when one is coming downhill from behind you. If your dog is in front of you, let the bicyclist know that there is a dog ahead of him. When the bicyclists go uphill, they do not want to lose their momentum. Do not let your dog bother the bicyclists.

During *hunting season*, put bright hunter orange on your dog. Dog vests are available from Valley Feed and local hunting supply stores; if you do not get a vest for him, buy a fluorescent collar or tie a bright hunter orange ribbon around his neck. It just might save his life, especially if he is a large dog that could be mistaken for a deer (like "Toby," my Weimaraner).

Although rare, poison bait and leghold traps are a few of the other hazards your dog might encounter. These are usually on private property and you are unlikely to encounter either on any of the hikes in this book.

"Outside of a dog, a book is a man's best friend; and inside a dog, it's too dark to read."   *Mark Twain*

10   Emergency Treatments When Hiking

by Judy F. Eddy

Although hiking with your dog is usually trouble-free, accidents can happen. If you have a first-aid kit with you, both you and your dog will be better off. Bleeding after being stabbed by a broken branch or breaking a bone in a fast run over a cliff edge can happen. If you encounter any of the listed emergency situations, get to a veterinarian fast. These emergency hints are no substitute for a veterinarian's care. However, these stopgap measures might help until you can get professional treatment for your dog.

Unfortunately, first-aid courses for animals are almost exclusively for animal care workers. However, any first-aid course for humans is going to give you greater confidence when it comes to dealing with any emergencies your dog might experience. While everything might not translate, many techniques do. Those could be the ones that save your dog's life.

Always speak to your wounded dog in a calm, reassuring voice. Approach him with caution. It might be necessary to use a muzzle if he is snapping in panic. However, if your dog is in shock, use a muzzle only as a last resort. You might have to open his breathing passage, and you do not have time to waste with a muzzle.

To improvise a muzzle, wrap a wide piece of adhesive tape around his snout. Do not bind it too tightly. You can also use a strip of cloth, a belt or even your hiking sock, wrapped snugly around his muzzle and tied off behind his ears.

Eye Injury

If your dog injures an eye, or starts squinting or blinking, **do not wait** to take him to the veterinarian. Eye injuries are usually easily treated, but even minor ones should be looked at immediately. Eye infections can progress very quickly.

Bleeding From External Wounds

Almost any bleeding (even spurting arterial wounds) can be controlled by the direct pressure method. Press gauze, cling-free cloth or even your hand over the wound and maintain firm pressure. If the bleeding does not stop, increase the pressure. Check the bleeding in 5 or 10 minutes by releasing the pressure. Do not remove the cloth, since this could open the wound.

If the wound is still dripping, continue direct pressure. If necessary, muzzle your dog.

Do not panic. Sometimes a little blood can look like a lot. Stay calm. Get your dog to a veterinarian immediately. If you are transporting him by yourself and cannot maintain pressure by hand, bandage the cloth firmly in place. Always check for shock and treat that if necessary (see below). If your dog is unconscious, elevate his hind end so blood can get to his brain.

Gravity can also help. If the wound is in the front leg, try to stand your dog on his hind legs while you treat him. This raises the wound above the heart, and should slow the bleeding.

For bleeding from fractures that protrude through the skin, apply pressure between the break and your dog's heart, slightly above the injury. For a compound fracture of the lower leg, tightly encircle your dog's upper leg with your hands.

Veterinarians advise against tourniquets except in the most dire circumstances. Many say there is rarely a situation when you will have to use one. If a tourniquet is done improperly, lack of circulation can cause your dog to lose a limb. But if you have tried direct pressure and the arterial bleeding is still profuse, and it looks like a matter of life over limb, you might need to make a tourniquet.

To do so, place a two-inch-wide clean strip of cloth or gauze slightly above the wound, over the bleeding artery. Tightly wrap it twice around the limb, and tie a stick into the wrap. Twist the stick until the bleeding is controlled. Secure the stick in place with tape. Cover your dog loosely with a blanket and get to a veterinarian immediately.

Broken Bones

If you are within a short drive of a veterinarian, it might be best to carefully transport your dog (see below) and let the veterinarian take care of the injury. Some veterinarians say they have seen more harm than good done by improperly applied splints.

Consider muzzling your dog. Most broken bones are extremely painful, and the pain combined with the stress your dog feels might cause him to bite you, even though you are best buddies.

If you are on a long hike, or far from immediate medical care, you might need to make a temporary support for the fracture. Treat only fractures of the lower leg. If you suspect fractures or dislocations elsewhere, carry him to a veterinarian as gently as possible (see below).

If bones protrude, control the bleeding with direct or encircling pressure (see above).

Wrap his leg with cloth or cotton batting. Place rigid sticks, such as tongue depressors, on opposite sides of the break so that they extend past joints at both ends of the break. Wrap with adhesive tape. Be sure not to wrap too tightly because a lack of circulation might result in loss of your dog's limb. See a veterinarian immediately.

Heat Stroke

Heat stroke is life-threatening, but its prevention is simple. You can avoid most heat stroke by keeping your dog in a cool, shady, well ventilated area, not exhausting him in hot weather, and providing lots of fresh water.

Never, ever leave your dog in a car on a warm day. Heat stroke generally occurs at temperatures greater than 100° but can often happen at much lower temperatures. Although the temperature outside might be tolerable, your car can become an oven, even with the windows partly open — and even in the shade.

The problem can happen when you park your car on a hot day to run into a shop for five minutes, and it takes a little longer than expected. You come back, and your dog is in big trouble, even if the window is cracked open.

Symptoms of heat stroke are rapid panting, bright red gums, high body temperature, and hot limbs. If your dog tries to walk, he might appear to be wobbling. Symptoms can progress to uncontrollable diarrhea, collapse and coma. As with people, death can occur in severe cases.

Use any method possible to cool your dog. In mild cases, it is often effective to move him to a cool, well ventilated place and wrap him in a cold, wet towel. But treatment generally calls for bathing him in cold water. Ice is especially effective when packed around the head. If your dog has heat stroke symptoms, treat him immediately. Rapid treatment is essential because your dog's condition can deteriorate quickly. Rush to a veterinarian immediately.

Shock

Shock is insufficient blood flow caused by problems with the heart, or loss of blood volume. It can result from injury or overwhelming infection. If prolonged, it can lead to death.

Symptoms of shock are pale gums, weak faint pulse, general weakness, shallow rapid breathing, listlessness or confusion, low body temperature or shivering, semiconsciousness or unconsciousness.

Do not muzzle your dog unless snapping becomes a danger to you.

Control any bleeding (see above). If your dog is unconscious, keep his airway open by opening his mouth and carefully pulling out his tongue. If he is conscious, let him relax and assume the position most comfortable for him. An ideal position is on his side with his head extended, but do not force him into it. Cover him lightly with a blanket and transport him immediately to a veterinarian.

Porcupine Quills

If your dog goes after a porcupine and comes to you with quills in his face, keep him calm. Try to keep him from pawing at his face. If he has even one quill inside his mouth, it is likely that there are others in there. Get him to the veterinarian.

If there are just a few quills on his nose or muzzle, you can use the needlenose pliers in your first-aid kit to pull them out. With the pliers, grab the quill as close to your dog's fur as possible. Using gentle pressure, pull the quill out quickly. Because the quills are barbed, this can hurt your dog so he might cry out. If it is too painful for him, leave the rest and go to the veterinarian for help. If you are able to remove the quills without too much protest from your dog, feel him for any quills that might be hidden in his fur, especially on his neck, chest, and inside of his legs and paws.

If any quills break as you try to pull them out, take your dog to a veterinarian. Leaving them in can cause infection and the veterinarian will need to remove them.

If your dog is covered with quills, promptly head back to your car and get him to a veterinarian right away.

After the quills have been removed, monitor your dog for three to four days for swelling, redness, weeping or other signs of infection. If you notice any of these, take him to the veterinarian right away.

Cuts from Ski Edges

When you are crosscountry or backcountry skiing with your dog, it is important that you watch out for his feet and legs. Sometimes your dog will run in front of you or another skier. Skis have edges that can cut. Your dog can suffer a deep gouge that can cut a tendon, muscle, or blood vessels. If the injury is more than superficial, treat it as a bleeding wound with a compression wrap/pressure bandage and get him to the veterinarian as soon as you can get back to your car.

Snares and Traps

Snares and traps are usually set on private property rather than along any of the hikes described in this book. Most traps are set to catch beaver, muskrat, bobcat, coyote, fox, pine marten, and raccoons. Three types are used: Leghold traps grab the animal by the foot or leg; Conibear and other killer traps crush or strangle the animal; and snares can be of the neck or foot variety.

If your dog does come upon a snare or trap and gets his face, neck or foot caught, you should carefully open the jaws of the trap or cut the snare wire with wire cutters. The Conibear and other killer traps require both hands to squeeze the springs that line the sides. If you know how to open it, you have from 3 to 8 minutes to stop your dog from suffocating.

If you cannot remove a nonlethal trap or snare from your dog, unanchor it and bring it and the dog to a veterinarian immediately.

Poison Bait

If your dog eats some poison bait, take him to a veterinarian immediately. If you are hours away from the car, you should immediately try to get him to vomit. If your first-aid kit includes hydrogen peroxide, give him 1-3 teaspoons (depending on his size) every 10 minutes until he vomits.

If you carry syrup of ipecac in your first-aid kit, you can use it to induce vomiting. You do not need much. Veterinarians use 3-6 milliliters, depending on the size of the dog. For a small dog, use about 1/2 teaspoon and for a larger dog, use about 1 teaspoon. If vomiting does not occur within 20 minutes, repeat the dose once.

Alternatively, you can try to absorb the poison in his stomach with tablets or capsules of activated charcoal. The dose is 2 grams for every 2.2 pounds of your dog's body weight. Thus, if your dog weighs approximately 35 pounds, give him approximately 35 grams, and give your 75-pound dog approximately 75 grams.

In either case (if you induce vomiting or attempt to absorb the poison), get your dog to the veterinarian immediately. If possible, bring with you a sample of the bait and your dog's vomit so it can be tested for ingredients.

Antifreeze

You should know that the antifreeze used in automobiles is poisonous to your dog. When you are in a parking lot before or after your hike, be especially alert to any puddles your dog might decide to drink from. The active ingredient in antifreeze, ethylene glycol, has a sweet taste that appeals to your dog even though it is toxic (it can cause kidney failure). If your dog does lick any antifreeze, it is an immediate emergency. Take him to the veterinarian so he can be given an antidote.

Hit by a Car

If your dog is hit by a car, you must get him to a veterinarian immediately. Because your dog might try to bite you if he is in pain or shock, use a muzzle if he is conscious. Stay calm and talk to him in a soothing voice.

If he is unconscious or unable to move, make a stretcher with a board, blanket or coat. Slide him onto it and get him into the car and drive to the veterinarian immediately. If he is bleeding, apply direct pressure and a pressure bandage. To help prevent shock, cover him with a blanket, jacket or sweater. Even if he appears to be uninjured, have a veterinarian check him because he could have internal injuries.

Transporting an Injured or Ill Dog

It is best to use a stretcher to move your dog if he cannot walk to avoid worsening any injury. A good makeshift stretcher is a large, sturdy board, but a blanket or even a rug will do. Carefully slide your dog onto the stretcher, making sure not to bend any part of his body. On a board stretcher, tie him gently, but firmly, in place. The goal is to move the dog in one piece with a minimal amount of motion.

Again, muzzle him if he is in pain. You will not be able to safely drive him to the veterinarian if he has bitten you.

After you get your dog into the vehicle, speak reassuringly to him enroute to the veterinarian.

No man can be condemned for owning a dog. As long as he has a dog, he has a friend; and the poorer he gets, the better friend he has."
Will Rogers

11 Jackson Hole Community Pathways

by Margie Lynch

The Jackson Hole Community Pathways system is a wonderful place to enjoy time with your dog. Beginning in 1995, pathways sections have been constructed in several locations throughout Jackson Hole to provide close-to-home, non-motorized transportation and recreation options for Jackson Hole's residents and visitors. The sections connect to form a valley-wide system of trails and all feature the beautiful scenery that makes Jackson Hole so special.

The pathways are paved, shared-use facilities and are enjoyed by walkers, runners, equestrians, bicyclists, in-line skaters, and nordic skiers. Motorized uses are prohibited. Users are asked to be considerate of others to ensure the enjoyment of all.

The same multiple-use guidelines that apply to Forest Service trails also apply to the pathways. Bicyclists yield to pedestrians, who yield to horseback riders. That is, horseback riders always have the right of way, you and your dog have the right of way over bicyclists and skaters. In-line skaters are treated the same as bicyclists for these purposes. Generally, courtesy should govern all interactions. In particular, people approaching from the rear are encouraged to verbally or by means of a bell alert people ahead of them to their presence.

Because the pathways are a transportation corridor for bicyclists, do not expect bikers to slow for your off leash dog. Stay alert so that you can protect your dog.

Pathways Dog Rules

Dog control is the responsibility of the owner. Dogs are required to be under physical control in sections so signed. This means that your dog must be on a leash. Currently, the only section with this stipulation for dog control is the Russ Garaman Trail between the post office in west Jackson and the first bridge that crosses Flat Creek. On all other pathways sections, it is required that dogs be under voice or physical control. Dog owners who violate these rules can be subject to fines up to $750.

As a courtesy to other pathways users, you are asked to clean up after your dog. Plastic bags (Mutt Mitts) and trash receptacles are provided along the pathways for your convenience.

Trail Sections

The Russ Garaman Trail, School Trail, and Indian Springs Trail

Directions and Parking: To reach the beginning of the pathway in Jackson, take Maple Way or Powderhorn Lane off West Broadway Avenue. On-street parking is available for pathway users behind the post office on Maple Way. An alternative parking site is at the High School or Middle School. Parking is not permitted on Highway 22.

These three trail sections form more than three continuous miles between Jackson and Wyoming Highway 22. From its beginning near the post office in west Jackson, the Russ Garaman Trail winds next to Flat Creek, crossing it at several locations by means of beautiful wooden bridges. The Crabtree Bridge connects Crabtree Lane in West Jackson with the Russ Garaman Trail. There is a tunnel under Highway 89, connecting the Russ Garaman Trail with the School Trail. After passing the Jackson Hole High School and Middle School, the School Trail becomes the Indian Springs Trail, where trail users take in impressive views of the Teton Range across the open space adjacent to the Indian Trails Subdivision.

This trail is groomed for winter use between the Jackson Hole High School and the post office (approximately 2 miles).

Miles (one way): 3.2
Difficulty: Easy (mostly level)

Melody Ranch Trail

Directions and Parking: The Melody Ranch Trail is located 5.5 miles south of the Jackson Town Square along Highway 89. The pathway starts at South Park Loop, just after the right turn off Highway 89. Parking for this section is located past the beginning of the pathway. Turn right on the dirt road where you see several utility boxes and park on the gravel open area across from the boxes. A few parking spaces at the south end of the pathway can be found in the paved open area at the start of Game Creek Road. The southern end of the pathway is located directly across the highway from this road. Please observe all "No Parking" signs.

The Melody Ranch Trail, completed in the fall of 1997, is a scenic 2-mile pathway that meanders next to ranch land and wildlife habitat, with views of the Snake River and Teton Ranges.

There are several challenging hills on the trail, making for an excellent outing if fitness is your goal.

Miles (one way): 2
Difficulty: moderate to difficult

Teton Pines/Moose-Wilson Trail

Directions and Parking: The best place to park to use this pathway is at its north end. From its intersection with Highway 22, travel 2.3 miles on the Teton Village Road (Highway 390) and turn left onto Kennel Lane at the sign for the Aspens and Jackson Hole Racquet Club Resort. The pathway begins across from the Jackson State Bank.
This one-mile pathway section connects commercial and residential development at the Aspens and Teton Pines with the new Wilson firehouse along the Teton Village Road (Highway 390).

Funding is available to construct an additional 7 miles of this pathway. Construction should be undertaken in the next several years.

Miles (one way): 1
Difficulty: Easy

The Wilson Centennial Trail

Directions and Parking: The Centennial Trail is located north of Highway 22 west of the Teton Village Road (Highway 390). Parking is available at the elementary school and in the big gravel lot on the left side of the Teton Village Road just north of its intersection with Highway 22. While these areas are under construction, please park with consideration for other activities.
The Wilson Centennial Trail commemorates the 100th anniversary of the Town of Wilson in 1995. This 1.2-mile trail connects the new Wilson School on the east end of Wilson with the Teton Village Road (Highway 390). A spur provides residents of Fish Creek Road with a shortcut to the pathway through the Wilson Meadows subdivision. The route roughly parallels Highway 22. This trail is groomed in the winter.

In Wilson, be sure to explore the marsh project constructed by the Jackson Hole Land Trust, where you are sure to find interesting wetland wildlife and vegetation. Although there is not at present a leash law in effect for the marsh project, the

Land Trust hopes there will not be problems with dogs flushing and chasing the wildlife. The trail is not directly adjacent to sensitive areas in the marsh. However, please take special care with your dog in this area, using a leash if necessary to control your dog. An observation platform at one place in the marsh allows you to see the entire project from above.

<u>Miles</u> (one way): 1.2 plus two spurs, totaling another 3/4 mile
<u>Difficulty</u>: Easy

Paul Merritt Trail (South Highway 89)

<u>Directions and Parking</u>: To reach the beginning of the path-
   way in Jackson, park at the High School or Middle School.
   To travel north from the southern end, follow the directions for the Melody Ranch Trail and park there.
This four-mile pathway section along South Highway 89
connects the Russ Garaman Trail just north of the Flat Creek
underpass with the von Gontard Trail to Melody Ranch Trail.
You can now go more than 7 miles one way without riding on
the street! Kids at Rafter J and Melody Ranch can now ride
safely to school on this pathway, off the highway.

<u>Miles</u> (one way): 4
<u>Difficulty</u>: Moderate

Old Henry's Road Trail

Directions and Parking: Follow the directions for the Melody
   Ranch Trail. You can park at Game Creek Road or at the
   Melody Ranch parking area.
A pathway south of town is available for residents who live along
the Henry's Road above Porcupine Creek or Game Creek. The
gravel trail connects the southern end of the Melody Ranch Trail
to the Old Henry's Road near Squaw Creek, providing access to
town along the Melody Ranch Trail. Access to the Game Creek
and Cache Creek trails is also available , allowing users to avoid
crossing the Snake River on the South Park bridge. Eventual
plans call for its extension to Hoback Junction.

<u>Miles</u> (one way): half-mile
<u>Difficulty</u>: Moderate

Winter Pathways Use

The Parks and Recreation Department grooms for winter use, when conditions permit, the Game Creek, Cache Creek/Hagen, Garaman and School, Melody Ranch, and Wilson trails, as well as the northeast side of the Snake River levee.

When using these trails with your dog, please preserve a good surface for nordic skiers. Remember that the purpose of the grooming is for skiing. Show consideration for the skiers by staying out of the ski tracks and keeping your dog out of them, also.

Also, please direct your dog to go off the main trail surface to make his poops in order to preserve an enjoyable experience for winter users and to ease spring cleaning efforts. If your dog does make a poop on the groomed surface, use a Mutt Mitt to pick it up, or use a stick, your shoe or boot, your ski pole, or whatever, to move it off the trail.

Future Pathways

Funds to design and conduct environmental reviews for a pathway connecting Wilson and Victor Idaho have been received. The Old Pass Road will be the probable route on the eastern side of the range. In the early 21st century, pathways users will be able to travel between Wilson Wyoming and Victor Idaho on the 17-mile Teton Pass Trail.

The Highway 22 Pathway will connect the Indian Springs Trail and the Moose-Wilson Trail along Highway 390. The Moose-Wilson Trail should also be constructed at about the same time. The County will oversee the design of this pathway along the Village Road.

The Town of Jackson has received a grant in federal transportation funds from the Wyoming Department of Transportation to plan a pathway along Flat Creek. The study area includes the Karns Meadow and north Flat Creek from the bridge at the 5-way stop sign to the North Cache Visitors Campus.

Information

For more information about the Jackson Hole Community Pathways system and how you can help bring more trails to Jackson Hole, contact

Friends of Pathways
PO Box 2062
Jackson
(307) 733-4534
email: fop@jhinet.com

You can get individual trail maps at our website:
http://www.jhpathways.org

12 Jackson Area Hikes

by Lorene Bagley

The County Pathways System is great for a walk but if you want to take a longer, dog-friendly hike, this chapter provides information about the
• length
• elevation gain
• availability of water for your dog
• how to get there
• a short description of the hike itself

Areas Covered in this Chapter

Town of Jackson
Teton Range
Gros Ventre Range
Snake River Range
Big Hole Range

Rating System for the Hikes

This book provides a two-part rating system. It rates the hike for the humans for difficulty and length, and interesting terrain. But, most important, the system rates the hikes for your dog — availability of water, likelihood of wildlife or bicycles, and opportunities for socializing with other dogs.

The human rating system is fairly straightforward; for it, words best describe the difficulty and length. Bones are used for the dog's rating system. Most of the hikes will have quite a few bones. This is because we try to take our dogs on hikes that they will enjoy, and that have ample water for them.

The rating system also provides information about the best (or worst) time of year for the hike, and whether the trail is dog friendly in the winter months.

When trying to understand mountain topography, it helps to first look to the valleys and then move upland. Jackson's Hole, which lies within Teton County, is surrounded by the Teton Range on the west, the Gros Ventre (pronounced "grow vont") on the east, and the Snake River Range to the south. West of the Teton Range lies Teton Valley, formerly known as Pierre's Hole. To its west lies the Big Hole Mountain Range, a wonderful low elevation chain of mountains with little bear activity.

West of Jackson is the majestic Teton Range, home to Grand Teton National Park. Much of this range lies within the park boundaries and is therefore off limits to your canine friend. However, many Teton Range hikes are accessible from Teton Valley. The western slope of the Teton Range is home to the Jedediah Smith Wilderness area and Targhee National Forest, very canine friendly indeed. Your dog is welcome east of Jackson in the Gros Ventre Range, with its highly visible "Sleeping Indian" (Sheep Mountain) and Jackson Peak, as well as south of Jackson in the Snake River Range. As a matter of fact, the National Forests are extremely friendly and accessible for you to walk your dog.

Well, that is put in very simple terms. Get a map, and a good hiking guide. I recommend in particular those by Rebecca Woods. She describes hikes that are detailed and highly informative, with much history thrown in, and some of the hikes are dog-friendly. Check the weekly newspapers for columns about area hikes. Keith Watts, who writes about hikes as a geologist for the "Jackson Hole News," also tells whether "Best Dog Brooks" has enjoyed the hike.

Familiarize yourself with the topography of the area you explore. Take it upon yourself to learn where you are. Getting lost is not a pleasant experience. As a safety precaution, you would be wise to have pepper spray with you when you hike. It will deter bear and moose, and might save your and your dog's lives.

The hikes I have included as "canine friendly" provide wonderful opportunities to explore the solitude of the Snake River Range, the awe-inspiring Teton Range, and the remarkable Gros Ventre and Big Hole Ranges. And the best part is that all these hikes can include your best friends. Dogs are truly meant to be cherished. They sum up the very best in each and every one of us.

I can think of no greater joy than summiting a peak, and then giving my dog Chief a big kiss.

Happy Hiking!

Town of Jackson

You are fortunate in that many great dog-friendly hikes are quite close to downtown Jackson. Hikes covered in this section:

- Snow King Mountain

- Cache Creek

- Elk Refuge Road

- Snake River Levee

- Game Creek

Snow King Mountain

<u>Getting There</u>: parking lot at Cache Street and Snow King Avenue

<u>The Hike</u>: Extremely steep for the first third of the walk — do not try to keep up with your dog at this point. However, when the trail eases and you face only a moderate climb with switchbacks, you can walk with your dog and enjoy the walk and its views.

The trail is the ski area's dirt service road. It is easy to follow. Because the trail is so close to town, you will encounter many people walking the trail, some with dogs; you will see some people running; and a few hardy bicyclists. As with all encounters with bicyclists, especially those that are going downhill, keep your dog out of the way.

Switchbacks through forested slopes allow for easier walking. Your dog might notice the occasional squirrel. Or, he might flush a grouse. There is a nature trail at the top as well as hiking trails that take you south or west.

Most people walk down the same way they went up. However, you can take any of the other trails down. If you do, you will need to make arrangements for shuttling back to your car. You can walk down the Game Creek Trail or Leeks Canyon (both of these are on the backside of Snow King Mountain).

In the summer, Snow King Stables takes horseback riders across part of the trail, and your dog might be tempted to eat the horse manure. There is no water on this hike but in the summer, the kind folks at Panorama House put out a tub of water for the dogs. It is most welcome but you or your dog should carry water. This will help relieve the situation of scarce water by providing some for those dogs whose owners were not aware of its lack. In the early spring when the trail is first open for walking, there is an abundance of snow for your dog to roll in.

<u>Miles</u> (roundtrip): 3.2
<u>Elevation Gain</u>: 1571 feet

<u>Human Rating</u>
- spectacular views
- sociability
- short and quick
- good workout

<u>Canine Rating</u>
- no water
- bicyclists

Cache Creek

Getting There: From the Town Square, head east on Broadway Avenue, turn right on Redmond (opposite St John's Hospital) and drive south for five blocks. Make a left on Cache Creek Drive until you come to the Forest Service parking lot (1.2 miles). There is a well maintained outhouse at the parking lot.

The Hike: The trail starts on an old jeep road. Alternatively, there is a boardwalk that follows the creek for a short distance, with benches for sitting and enjoying the peaceful sound of the creek rippling (or roaring, depending on the time of the year).

Because the jeep road is wide enough for more than one person, this is a great hike to enjoy with a friend or two, allowing for plenty of good conversation. Hundreds of bicyclists, walkers and runners use this trail every day. At about half a mile, the road passes the Bar-T-Five Covered Wagon Cookout on the right and then starts a short uphill. The road alternates between level and slight uphills, going through open fields and treed areas.

Water is available all year for your dog, although in the spring the snowmelt can make the creek dangerous when it flows too fast. In the summer, there are a lot of bicyclists, and because of the Bar-T-Five Covered Wagon Cookout's horse-drawn wagon, there is horse manure on the road, which attracts a lot of bugs.

The best times of the year for walking are the spring and autumn. In the winter, because the trail is groomed, it is ideal for cross country skiing or snowshoeing; however, be alert for snowmobiles.

After approximately two miles, the jeep road ends and turns into a regular forest trail. Many people turn around here. However, if you continue on this trail, you might choose to take the turnoff to Game Creek Trail. In that case, you will need to have a car at the end of Game Creek Trail.

Or, you can stay on Cache Creek Trail and climb to Cache Creek Pass. From there, you can choose from any number of different trails, one of which goes to Curtis Canyon and Goodwin Lake.

Miles: depends on how far you go; a natural turnaround at the end of the jeep road is approximately 2 miles from the parking area. You can go approximately 9 miles to the boundary of the Bridger Wilderness and then beyond into the Gros Ventre Mountains. Or, you can go to the Game Creek parking area (approximately 6 miles).

Elevation Gain: depending on how far you go, a few hundred feet to the end of the jeep road before the start of the single trail or approximately 730 feet if you make the Cache Creek/ Game Creek circuit

Human Rating

- gentle terrain
- close to town
- sociability

Canine Rating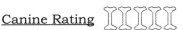

- plenty of water
- lots of other dogs
- many bicyclists
- winter use
- snowmobiles in winter

Humans have 5 million scent receptors; dogs have 220 million scent receptors. However, your dog's ability to smell is one hundred thousand to one hundred million times better than yours.

Elk Refuge Road

Getting There: Drive east on Broadway Avenue until you reach the end. Park at the left turn area at the entrance to the Elk Refuge.

The Hike: This is not so much a hike as a nice place to walk. Your dog is welcome as long as he stays on the road with you. He is definitely NOT allowed to chase the elk, and you will want to be sure he does not harass the mountain lions, coyotes or wolves. He can be shot if you let him run off the road.
The walk stays on the road, has no shade but is convenient to town. However, cars do use this road and in the summer many tourists drive the road in the hope that they will see some wildlife. Mountain lions have been seen on the elk refuge.

Miles: as far as you want, depending on the time of year
Elevation Gain: none

Human Rating
- close to town
- can walk two or more abreast
- some vehicular traffic

Canine Rating
- no water
- must stay on the road
- wildlife

Snake River Levee

Getting there: From the town of Jackson, drive west on Broadway Avenue and turn right onto Highway 22, heading toward Wilson. When you reach the Snake River, you can park
on the northeast side at Emily's Pond in a well maintained
parking lot with trash receptacles. Alternatively, you can
cross the river and park on the southwest side. There is an
outhouse on the northwest side of the bridge. Although you
can park here, most of the spaces are taken by boaters.

The Hike: This is another local favorite for a quick walk, run,
bike ride or crosscountry ski with your dog. The northeast
and southwest sections of the levee are open to the public.
You will meet many other people and dogs as you head toward the closed gate at the end of each of these sections.
You will also see birds: ducks, swans, eagles, blackbirds,
bluebirds, and others. Moose are abundant in the winter,
and are browsing in the willows even in the summer.
No matter which of the two sections you choose, the directions
for each are rather straightforward. From the parking area, proceed on the dirt road until you come to a closed gate, past which
you would be trespassing. On both sides the distance is about 2
miles one way.

If you go on the northeast section, you will pass a few ponds
that are great swimming holes for your dog. Of course, he can
also enjoy the water in various sections of the river. During the
late summer and autumn, there is a closed gate at approximately 1-3/4 miles when the Walton cattle are grazing beyond
it. However, if the gate is open and you go beyond it, the road
splits and you can take either way until you reach a final closed
gate (approximately a quarter to a half mile). Because there is a
working quarry beyond this last closed gate, the northeast levee
is sometimes closed when heavy trucks use it. However, this
also makes for a road that is rather well groomed. However, the
northeast side of the levee is notorious for burrs, especially in
late summer and autumn.

If you go on the southwest section, there are a few ponds,
as well as sections in the river, in which your dog can swim.
During the fishing season in particular, car traffic can make
this section undesirable.

Both sections are good for winter crosscountry skiing or
snowshoeing. However, dogs who normally make their poops
well off the side of the levee at other times of the year do not do
this in the winter. Most try to avoid the ski tracks but do not

always manage. Keep your eyes open — if your dog does poop in the ski track, be considerate and use a Mutt Mitt, your ski pole or a twig to move it out of the track.

Miles (one way): about 2 on either side of the river
Elevation Gain: none

Human Rating	Canine Rating 
• close to town and flat	• lots of water
• can walk two or more and abreast	• burrs in the late summer autumn
• no regular vehicular traffic on northeast side (Emily's Pond) but with quarry work, this side is not always available.	• moose in the winter
	• vehicles on southwest
	• winter use

Your dog's eyes are 10 times more sensitive than human eyes to peripheral movements. Thus, your dog can spot a slight movement in the bushes that you would never see. So, when he runs off after "nothing," it could very well be something that you cannot see.

Game Creek

<u>Getting there</u>: From town, head west on Broadway Avenue to the "Y" (the intersection of Broadway Avenue and Highway 22, with Buffalo Junction). From the "Y," drive 6 miles south on Highway 89 to the left hand turn. Drive about another mile to the parking area at the base of a hill; follow the signs.

<u>The Hike</u>: You can reach the saddle between Game Creek and Cache Creek and turn around, or you can continue to the parking lot at the start of the Cache Creek trail.

The lower part of the trail is in a drainage, and is relatively gentle. The trail passes a few beaver ponds, and eventually a small spring, providing water for your dog. From here, you climb steadily until you reach the saddle. Wildflowers are abundant in the summer. Mountain lion have been seen in the Game Creek area. Many bicyclists make a circuit with the Cache Creek Trail so stay alert and be cooperative. They usually do not go as fast on this trail as they do on Cache Creek, however.

The lower part of the trail is quite good for winter crosscountry skiing or snowshoeing.

<u>Miles</u>: depends on how far you go; you can turn back at any time. Alternatively, you can make an approximate 10-mile circuit with Cache Creek (you will need to shuttle a car).

<u>Elevation Gain</u>: depends on how far you go; the elevation at the saddle between Game Creek and Cache Creek is 7410 feet

<u>Human Rating</u>	<u>Canine Rating</u> 
• pleasant walk	• water
• wildflowers	• bicyclists
	• winter use

East of Jackson (Gros Ventre Range)

The Gros Ventre range is located to the east of Jackson Hole. Its most visible peaks are "Sleeping Indian" (Sheep Mountain) and Jackson Peak.

It has many hikes for those who are interested. Check trail books for hikes other than those described here. Because the area is Forest Service, you can take your dog anywhere. However, some of the summer hiking areas are closed during the winter to protect winter wildlife from stress. Maps of closed areas are available from the Forest Service.

It is also important to note that the Gros Ventre Range is home to the occasional black bear. BE AwaRe. Talk to your buddy; make noise. This is your best defense.

Hikes included in the Gros Ventre Range:

- Goodwin Lake and Jackson Peak

- Gros Ventre Slide Interpretive
    Trail/Lower Slide Lake

- Blue Miner Lake

- Ditch Creek

- Shadow Mountain

"I go to the hills, when my heart is lonely. And I'll sing ... again."
Lorene Bagley

Goodwin Lake and Jackson Peak

Getting There: Take Broadway Avenue east to the end and turn
    left onto the Elk Refuge Road. After approximately one mile,
    turn right at the signed road. Drive this switchbacking dirt
    road up the hill, passing the turnoff to Curtis Canyon Camp-
    ground at 7.5 miles. Bear right at 9.2 miles. The left road
    leads to Sheep Creek Road. The parking area at the trailhead
    is reached approximately 10 miles from the Elk Refuge en-
    trance and is easy to recognize. The road to the parking area
    is not in the best condition; four-wheel drive is recommended.

The Hike: Located within the Bridger-Teton National Forest,
    Goodwin Lake is a wonderful easy-to-moderate hike that
    ends at a gorgeous alpine lake. This wilderness area hike
    has no mountain bikers who can come around a turn too
    fast and hit your dog. There can be bugs in the summer, so
    carry a repellant. A grizzly bear was seen at the lake in the
    summer of 1999 so be sure you have your bear spray when
    you hike here.
The well defined dirt trail heads north on the slope from where
you parked. Making one large switchback, you then head south
to the ridgeline. You walk along the ridge and climb steeply
through a wonderful towering pine forest. Here is a place to
walk softly and listen to the abundance of wildlife activity. You
soon realize that the downed trees all around have turned this
area into a bustling "city" of bird activity.

    The trail continues southward on a narrowing ridge. Shortly
after, the trail opens to an early growth meadow and beautiful
Teton views can be seen to your right. The trail then heads into
the forest. As the Teton views to your right disappear, the equally
beautiful Sheep Mountain (Sleeping Indian) comes into view on
your left. The trail heads southeast along the eastern side of the
hill on which you have been hiking.

    After a moderate grade through old forest you enter the
Gros Ventre Wilderness area, well marked by a sign. Please do
not mirror the careless people who have permanently scarred
the trees with their ignorant graffiti. The trail skirts the left side
of the hill and crosses a rocky landslide, then parallels the creek
that runs out of Goodwin Lake. Hiking around the lake is an
appealing option for those who have the time.

    Jackson Peak can be summited by continuing on the trail
left of Goodwin Lake. After about a mile across open meadows,
on the west you will see the east ridge of Jackson Peak. There is

no obvious trail but you can walk up the steep slopes to the crest of the ridge, and on to the rocky summit of 10,741 feet.

<u>Miles</u> (roundtrip): approx. 6
<u>Elevation Gain</u>: approx. 880 feet to Goodwin Lake

Human Rating

- long drive on rough dirt road
- beautiful views

Canine Rating

- water at creek
- water at lake
- bears

Your dog's internal clock has been measured to be accurate within 1 minute in a 24-hour cycle. Thus, you will notice that his demands for food or exercise are at the same time each day.

Gros Ventre Slide Interpretive Trail/Lower Slide Lake

Getting There: From downtown Jackson, drive north on Cache
Street to the Gros Ventre Junction and turn right toward
Kelly. About a mile past Kelly, turn right on the road marked
Kelly Hot Springs. Please don't let your dog swim in the hot
springs; he can pollute it for bathers. Drive approximately
4.5 miles further to the pullout marked Gros Ventre Slide
Geological Area.

The Hike: There are those days when a beautiful drive and swim
for your dog are enough. For these times, the beautiful drive
past Kelly to Lower Slide Lake is just perfect. The almost
half-mile interpretive trail points out common flora of the
region: Douglas fir, lodgepole pine, etc. If other people are
walking on this trail, be sure to have your dog under voice
control or put him on a leash. Some of the trail is on rock
and you do not want your dog to cause anyone to have an
accident.
Lower Slide Lake becomes visible almost immediately. You can
find a nice route to scramble to the lake so your dog can have a
pleasant swim. Or, you can return to your car and drive a little
further to find a private area for your dog to take a dip.

Miles (roundtrip): approx. 3.2
Elevation Gain: approx. 720 feet

Human Rating

- beautiful drive
- short hike
- interpretive trail
  explains the geological
  phenomenon of May 27 1927

Canine Rating

- good swimming

*The canine field of vision is 250° degrees; the human field of vision is
only 180° degrees.*

Blue Miner Lake

Getting There: Drive north out of town on Cache Street to the Kelly turnoff at the Gros Ventre Junction. About a mile past Kelly, turn right on the road marked Kelly Hot Springs. Please don't let your dog swim in the hot springs; he can pollute it for bathers. Drive approximately 11.5 miles to the trailhead on the right side of the road opposite the Red Hills Campground. (After passing the boat ramp at Slide Lake, the road deteriorates.)

The Hike: The well defined trail goes up a hill, turns southwest and then climbs a bit before dropping down into what was the old trail. A creek provides water for your dog. The trail rises again and dips again before climbing steadily upwards through sagebrush. A short flat section is followed by switchbacks up to a hillside from which you start to get great views, especially of the Red Rock area. At three miles, after having walked through a meadow, you'll be on level terrain and heading east through more meadows and clumps of trees. Heading right and climbing another ridge, you can see West Miner Creek and Crystal Creek drainages down below. Climbing even higher, you will eventually be able to see Sheep Mountain (the Sleeping Indian) in the southwest, and the Tetons in the northwest. After another approximately one mile of climbing, you are on the edge of a steep drop off. If it is clear, you can see the Wind River Range from here to the east. At five and a half miles (approximately), you reach a clearing filled with wildflowers (if you are hiking there at the right time of the year). Walking through more forest brings you to a meadow that is another mile long. The trail starts to fade but head toward the trees at the end of an amphitheater above the lake. At the trees, turn right and you will come to the trail that drops steeply about 600 feet to Blue Miner Lake (which means you must walk up this hill on your return).

Miles (one way): 7.5
Elevation Gain: 3370 feet

Human Rating
- long drive
- solitude
- great views and good workout

Canine Rating
- creek and lake water

Ditch Creek

Getting There: From downtown Jackson, drive north on Cache Street and turn right on Gros Ventre Road (6 miles). Drive for 9 miles (through Kelly) and turn right at the Teton Science School Road. Drive a further 3 miles on the Forest Service Road. In the winter you must park here because it is not plowed past this point. In the summer, drive about another fifth of a mile and park on the right.

The Hike: Walk on the dirt road, which follows Ditch Creek, for as long you as like. A good hike is about 4-5 miles one way. During this walk, there is plenty of water for your dog because the creek is always flowing. You can choose to take any of the many trails that branch off the road. Be alert for moose — they are attracted to the willows that grow in the creek. And in the late summer, bison have been seen in the area. This area is also good for biking, and it is terrific for crosscountry skiing in the winter.

Miles (one way): 4-5 miles for a nice walk
Elevation Gain: negligible

Human Rating

- pleasant in summer and winter
- can walk two or more abreast
- can bike or crosscountry ski

Canine Rating

- lots of water
- wildlife
- bicyclists
- winter use

Your dog has a direct connection from the nose to the brain areas for eating, drinking, and sex.

Shadow Mountain

Getting There: From downtown Jackson, drive north on Cache
Street and turn right on Gros Ventre Road. Continue through
Kelly and continue driving north until you come to the Forest Service sign and the parking area (passing the turnoff
for the Teton Science School). You can drive up Shadow
Mountain because the Forest Service maintains the road. In
the winter, however, you park about a mile from the base of
the mountain.

The Hike: Start your hike at the base of the mountain. Many
trees in the parking area provide shade for your car while
you are hiking. Walk on the road to the top. It is a steady
medium-to-hard climb. Because the hike follows the road,
it is a great opportunity for you and your friends to walk
side by side and have great conversations. Views are spectacular on a clear day. In midsummer, the wildflowers are in
full bloom and are outstanding. Vehicles do use the road so
watch out for them.
Many scenic single trails lead off the main road. If you see other
people on a side trail, you can ask if they know where the trail
ends, before you take it too far. You might end up back at the
parking area, but then again you might not and will have to
retrace your steps.

   In the winter, this is a favorite crosscountry ski area. When
you park here, note that the first mile or so to the base of the
mountain crosses through Grand Teton National Park. Your dog
must be on a leash for this section of packed base. You might
occasionally see bison along this flat section. Do NOT let your
dog chase them, or any other wildlife.

Miles (one way): approx 2.5
Elevation Gain: approx. 200 feet

Human Rating

• great views
• terrific in the winter
• can walk two or more abreast

Canine Rating

• no water
• vehicular traffic
• winter use

West of Jackson (Hiking from Wilson — Teton and Snake River Ranges)

The Teton and Snake River Ranges are located west of the Town of Jackson. Most of the eastern slopes of the Teton Range are in Grand Teton National Park.

Hikes included in the Teton Range:

• Phillips Canyon

• Old Pass Road and Crater Lake

• Ski Lake

• Ridgetop Trail/Black Canyon

Phillips Canyon

Getting There: From downtown Jackson, drive west on Broadway and turn right onto Highway 22 at the "Y." Drive west on Highway 22 to Wilson. Turn right on either First or West street to Main Street and then turn again onto Fish Creek Road. Drive approximately 3.1 miles and park on the right if space is available (room for about 3 cars), or drive another tenth of a mile and park on the left. Neither area has a sign so keep a sharp lookout. The parking area on the left is directly before a cattle guard.

If you park in the small area on the right, you have to cross the road to the trail. If you park on the left in the larger area, you will walk back along the road until you see the well defined trail on the right, opposite the small parking area.

The Hike: The hike is level at first, with the trail winding through trees and eventually following a creek, which must be crossed. If you are lucky, there will be some downed logs on which to do this, or you can ford it. There have been a few times when I have had to turn back because the water was flowing too fast to get across safely (usually during the spring thaw). The trail is fairly level for another half mile or so and then splits.

The right trail goes up Phillips Canyon, alternately climbing and leveling. It crosses the creek a few times, passes through a beautiful meadow, and eventually climbs through the forest to reach the junction of the trail that will take you to Ski Lake. At this junction, if you take the relatively flat trail to the left, you will come to the meadow area of the Ski Lake Trail at about the 1 mile mark. Take the trail straight and you will eventually come to Phillips Pass. Mountain bicyclists use this trail so stay alert.

Miles: depends on how far you go — if you go to the trail that takes you to Ski Lake, it is approximately 5 miles one way

Elevation Gain: depends on how far you go; if you go to Ski Lake, approximately 1500 feet

Human Rating
- relatively close
- steep
- can access Ski Lake

Canine Rating
- water in creek
- water at Ski Lake
- bicyclists
- moose

Old Pass Road and Crater Lake

Getting There: From downtown Jackson, drive west on Broadway and turn right onto Highway 22 at the "Y." Drive west
on Highway 22 through Wilson to Trail Creek Road on your
left, opposite the Heidelberg (1 mile after the Stagecoach in
Wilson). Stay on Trail Creek Road for 0.9 miles until it dead
ends at a gate; there is plenty of parking along both sides of
the road here.

The Hike: This hike follows the old paved road, although very
shortly after you start, a dirt trail branches off to the left.
You can take this to its end (just a short distance above
Crater Lake on the paved road). There is some water on this
dirt trail for your dog, with a creek that you will need to ford.
Because of trail erosion from bikes, this can sometimes be a
messy hike. One nice feature of the Old Pass Road itself is
that because it is paved, you don't have to walk in the mud.
About a mile after the gate at the parking lot, the moderately
climbing paved road brings you to a year-round spring that is
perfect for your dog on a hot summer day. This spring is also
available during the winter hikes up the Old Pass on your snowshoes. After about another quarter of a mile, you reach Crater
Lake. This is a gorgeous deep green lake. Across the lake, you
can see a permanent flow of water into the lake. As early as late
summer, the lake can be iced over; you do not want your dog to
fall into the lake through some ice so be careful. You also should
be careful because the log jams in the lake constantly move
around. However, in midsummer your dog will love swimming
here.

After a stop here, you might want to continue up the road.
On your left you will notice the dirt trail that returns to the
parking area. However, continuing to the top, the steep
switchbacks will get your heart pumping again. At the first
switchback, there is another spring for your dog, both on the
right side of the road (tunneling underneath to the left side) and
after the turn, on the left side before it tunnels under the road
on its way downhill. This is the last water until the top of the
road. If you continue to the summit, you will eventually join the
current Highway 22 Teton Pass Road. Just before you reach the
top, there is a year-round spring that provides drinking water
for your dog, enough to hold him until your return to Crater
Lake.

Watch out for moose all year on the Old Pass Road. They
used to be visible only during the winter months but recently

there have been a number of moose encounters during the summer. Bear scat has been seen on the road in late summer.

In the summer, many bicyclists use the Old Pass Road. Respect the fact that some are struggling to get up the hill and do not want your dog to bother them. However, they sometimes come down quite fast; although they should respect you and your dog's presence by slowing down, they do not always do this. Be prepared to call your dog to have him near when a bicyclist approaches. There have been encounters with bicyclists and dogs, and the dogs usually get scraped a little.

In the winter, especially on the weekends, the Old Pass Road has become a popular snowboarding and skiing site. Because they can come down the hill almost silently, it can be dangerous for your dog (or you). Thus, the Old Pass Road is not very dog-friendly in the winter. However, when the main highway is closed for avalanche blasting to remove dangerous snow, the snowboarders and skiers cannot drive to the top; use the opportunity to take your dog up the Old Pass Road. Because of the activity of the snowboarders and the skiers, the snow can be packed quite well.

<u>Miles</u> (roundtrip): approx. 3.4 to Crater Lake; approx. 8 to the top
<u>Elevation Gain</u>: approx. 1916 feet to the top

<u>Human Rating</u>

- beautiful views
- profuse wildflowers in the summer months
- sociability
- can walk two or more abreast
- relatively close

<u>Canine Rating</u>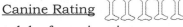

- lake for swimming
- skiers and snowboarders in the winter
- bicyclists
- winter use
- wildlife

Ski Lake

Getting There: From downtown Jackson, drive west on Broadway Avenue and turn right onto Highway 22 at the "Y." Drive through the town of Wilson and start to climb the Pass. At 3.8 miles after the Stagecoach Bar in Wilson, you will reach Phillips Canyon Road on the right. Pull in and park on the side of the dirt road. In the winter, the parking area is reached on the left at 3.6 miles after the Stagecoach in Wilson.

The Hike: The hike starts on a dirt road and soon crosses a year-round stream with water for your dog. Continue on the road until you come to a signed trail on the left. This moderate climb comes to a meadow that is filled with snowmelt water in the early summer. A footbridge crosses a creek that dries in the late summer. Continuing on the trail brings you to a signed junction: the right fork goes to Phillips Canyon and Phillips Pass; the left fork goes to Ski Lake. Taking the Ski Lake fork, the trail soon crosses another creek on a Forest Service bridge. The steep climb after the creek ends in a meadow before Ski Lake, after crossing an outflow of the lake. Bring mosquito repellant if you hike here in the summer.

A faint trail leads around the left side of the lake, where there are a few old campsites. A more defined trail leads you up and around the right side of the lake. Just a short distance up the right side gives you views of the beautiful emerald green Ski Lake, with the Gros Ventre Range behind. Continuing on up the trail brings you to a valley and the backside of the southernmost Teton Range comes into view. Gorgeous wildflowers reward those who explore the mountains surrounding Ski Lake.

Ski Lake is a popular hike for visitors and locals, and tends to get rather crowded. Usually, however, those who hike this trail have dogs. In spite of the crowds, it is still one of the best hikes for a short jaunt. Because you arrive at a beautiful alpine lake, your dog can swim here for hours. The lake is formed by former glaciers, set into a beautiful cirque.

Moose, as well as porcupines, can be encountered along this trail but there is little bear activity. In the winter, snowmobiles groom a trail but can disturb the peace of the forest. Sometimes, hunters from out of town are not aware of the heavy human and canine use on the trail, and you can hear gunshots in the area. Thus, in the autumn, it is best to be prepared by wearing hunter orange. Don't forget to protect your dog; put a hunter orange vest (made specifically for dogs) on him, or you can tie a hunter orange ribbon onto his collar.

<u>Miles</u> (roundtrip): approx. 4
<u>Elevation Gain</u> : approx. 760 feet

<u>Human Rating</u>

- a short hike to a
  beautiful alpine lake
- amazing views
- sociability
- relatively close
- can snowshoe or ski in the winter
  (you will need skins for the skis)

<u>Canine Rating</u>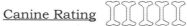

- plenty of water
- good swimming
- winter use

Consider that if your dog were flying in a biplane at an altitude of 300 feet over the city of Pittsburgh, he could smell 1 dissolved gram of butyric acid (a component of human sweat) in the air.

Ridgetop Trail/Black Canyon

Getting There: From downtown Jackson, drive west on Broadway Avenue and turn right onto Highway 22 at the "Y." Drive
through the town of Wilson and drive to the top of the Pass.
At the top, park on the left.

The Hike: The well marked trail off the parking area leads toward a communication tower. From there, the trail heads
south along the ridge. Alternating through trees and small
meadows, the trail crosses to a clearing at about two miles.
This is the turnaround for the ridgetop trail. You can continue up to the top of Peak 9279 for great views. There is a
sign at the turnaround for the Black Canyon trail.
Because there is no water on the Ridgetop Trail, you might
choose to go down Black Canyon. The trail drops about 1000
feet elevation in the first mile. Continuing down, you cross a
saddle and after about a half mile, the trail reaches Black
Canyon Creek. The creek provides water for your dog for the
rest of the hike. The trail goes through open areas and forested areas, constantly losing elevation. After narrowing, the
trail enters an open area and meanders to the parking area of
Old Pass Road/Crater Lake Trail. If there has been a lot of
rain, this area can be badly rutted from bicyclists. If you have
not shuttled a car, you can make a circular hike by walking
up the four miles of the Old Pass Road to the top of the Pass.
There is plenty of water.

Miles (one way): approx. 2 (to the turnaround); approx. 8 if
you add Black Canyon
Elevation Gain: approx. 760 feet; approx. 2685 feet descent if
you hike Black Canyon

Human Rating

• beautiful views
• not many people
• relatively close
• you can make a circular
12-mile hike

Canine Rating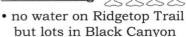

• no water on Ridgetop Trail
but lots in Black Canyon
• wildlife (e.g., moose)
• bicyclists

West of Teton Pass (Hiking east from Victor and Driggs — Teton Range)

The western slopes of the Teton Range are located across the Teton Pass in Teton Valley. For each of these hikes, drive over Teton Pass from Wilson. Dogs are welcome only on the western and southern slopes of the Teton Range. Home to Jedediah Smith Wilderness area and Winegar Hole Wilderness area, the northern Tetons are also home to both black and grizzly bears. BE AwaRe. Make noise and talk to your buddy as you hike any of these trails.

- Coal Creek and Taylor Mountain

- Mud Lake

- Darby Ice/Wind Caves

- The Wedge

- Peaked Mountain

- Pinnacle Trail

Coal Creek and Taylor Mountain

<u>Getting There</u>: From downtown Jackson drive west on Broadway and make a right turn onto Highway 22 at the "Y." Drive west on Highway 22 over Teton Pass toward Victor. The Coal Creek/Taylor Mountain turnout is on the right, near the bottom of the Pass (8.2 miles after the Stagecoach Bar in Wilson).

<u>The Hike</u>: The trail starts at a two-track dirt road just after a sign in the Coal Creek parking area. Shortly after is the Forest Service marker 008. The trail heads east to a footbridge that crosses Coal Creek. (Caution: the logs can be slippery.) The trail runs parallel to the left side of the creek. There are a series of Forest Service revegetation signs; please respect them.

After a modest to steep ascent, the trail crosses a tributary that is dry by late summer. It then leads through a beautiful aspen grove with about four steep switchbacks, leveling out in a gorgeous meadow sprinkled with beautiful wildflowers all summer. After crossing another tributary that is also dry by midsummer, the trail levels in a nice meadow where you rejoin Coal Creek. Water is always available here. The trail then heads due east where a signed junction gives you your hiking options. Head left to the summit of Taylor Mountain, or you can go straight to Mesquite Divide and continue to Phillips Pass. The last mile to the summit of Taylor Mountain is extremely steep at times. When the trail levels and gently ascends the saddle, you can either head up the rocky slope to the rock cairn or head up and over the saddle to Moose Meadows. Unless you have arranged a pickup or shuttled a car, you must retrace your steps back to the Coal Creek parking area. This trail is a good for your dog because there is water all summer.

Please respect the Grand Teton National Park rules by staying out of the Park with your dog. Although some beautiful hikes will be missed, you will be well rewarded with seclusion.

<u>Miles</u> (roundtrip): approx. 7.2
<u>Elevation Gain</u>: approx. 2788 feet

<u>Human Rating</u>
• views, in Wilderness Area

<u>Canine Rating</u>
• lots of water

Mud Lake

Getting There: From downtown Jackson drive west on Broadway and make a right turn onto Highway 22 at the "Y." Drive west on Highway 22 through Wilson and over Teton Pass onto Highway 33 through downtown Victor. At the end of downtown Victor (just before the Old Quilt House), turn right on Aspen Avenue. At 0.5 miles, turn left on Road 00. Another 0.2 miles further, turn right onto 7755. And, 0.4 miles further, park at the well signed Mud Lake Road and continue to hike on foot up the public road.

The Hike: Start on the public road at the foot of the hill. The hike follows the public road for the entire distance. At approximately a half to one mile, you can look to your right for a view of Victor (and the Teton Valley with the Big Hole Range beyond). Follow a steep series of switchbacks on the jeep road. Cross a cattle guard and crest the hill to Mud Lake, which is little more than a swampy pond, if not a man-made puddle.

Around the lake there is a jeep road and the ridgeline above shows wonderful Teton Valley views. The trail continues on to Baldy Knoll, which is a nice destination if you want to make a longer hike.

This trail can be accessed in the winter.

Miles (roundtrip): approx. 2.4 to Mud Lake; approx. 10 miles to Baldy Knoll
Elevation Gain: approx. 650 feet

Human Rating
• short hike
• good for birding

Canine Rating
• lots of water
• winter use

Humans have one to two feet of nasal membrane but your dog has 9 square yards of nasal membrane (more than his entire body surface).

Darby Ice/Wind Caves

Getting There: From downtown Jackson drive west on Broadway and make a right turn onto Highway 22 at the "Y." Drive
west on Highway 22 over Teton Pass from Wilson and onto
Highway 33 north from Victor toward Driggs. In Victor, set
your car's odometer. Turn right onto Forest Service road
012, just before the Spud Outdoor Theatre, 5.2 miles further. Continue straight until you reach a "T" in the road (at
1.6 miles). Take the right and follow it over a cattle guard
and then a left, entering the National Forest. Follow the road,
crossing two more cattle guards before taking a left at a
sign. The right route is a service entrance to the Darby Girls'
Camp, and is off limits. Follow the winding road for 6 miles
further, and park at the obvious trailhead parking lot where
the road deadends at the trailhead marked by a sign and a
map of the area.

The Hike: The trail takes you through a beautiful forest along
the south fork of Darby Canyon. There is a bench along the
trail near the beginning of the hike. Continue on the well
defined trail, heading up the heavily wooded left side of the
canyon. The trail switchbacks a few times.
You get your first glimpse of the Wind Cave across the canyon
when the trail opens up to wonderful views up Darby Canyon.
Because the Wind Cave is an amazing geological feature, it can
be rather crowded with people. It has slippery rocks that can be
sketchy for dog paws. Where the trail divides, stay right and
cross the creek; to reach the Wind Cave you follow the trail up
more steep switchbacks.
    At the junction, the route to the Ice Cave goes left, follow-
ing the creek for about a quarter mile where you take a right at
another junction. The Ice Cave is about half a mile further, up a
steep rocky slope.
    However, Chief and I stay out of all caves because Chief is
more comfortable outside on the trail. We just walk on the trail,
absorbing the nature that surrounds us, and then retrace our
steps back down to the car.

Miles (roundtrip): approx. 6.8 (Ice Cave); approximately 5.2
    (Wind Cave)
Elevation Gain : approx. 2410 feet (Ice Cave); approximately
    1870 feet (Wind Cave)

Human Rating

- long drive
- in Jedediah Smith Wilderness Area
- interesting geological attractions
- can be crowded

Canine Rating ⅠⅠⅠⅠ

- plenty of water
- slippery rocks at Wind Cave

Here is one area in which our senses exceed those of our dogs. Canines have 1700 taste buds but humans have 9000 buds.

The Wedge

<u>Getting There</u>: Follow the instructions to Darby Wind/Ice Caves, and begin your hike at an unmarked jeep trail to the left of the parking area.

<u>The Hike</u>: This is a steep climb with plenty of water and snow. An average winter snowfall still yields snow patches in mid-summer. The trail is well defined but unmarked on topographical maps. The hike begins on the left side of a parking area on an old jeep trail. You can see the jeep trail from the parking lot but must look for the single track dirt trail that heads off from the left of the jeep trail. If you reach a creek, you have missed the trail; turn around and look for the trail again.

Almost immediately after starting to hike, you begin on a well defined trail that heads left. Take this and cut through high overgrown vegetation (in the late summer) and cross numerous downed trees. After you start your ascent, you cross a small tributary where your dog can get a drink. The trail wastes no time at all climbing steeply up the canyon. There are points when the trail seems impossibly steep. After approximately 2 miles you cross another small spring — a trickle by late summer. Immediately after, there is a nice rock outcropping to take a break and soak in the views.

If you are at all unfamiliar with the surrounding mountains, bring a topo map for this hike. The Wedge is marked on the Mount Bannon Quadrangle Map, but the trail is not.

Directly across the canyon, Mt Meek, Mt Bannon, Mt Jedediah Smith and Fossil Mountain come into view. Continue up the moderate grade heading mainly east —toward the Tetons. The Wedge can be seen to your right. It looks father away than it actually is. The trail crosses an obvious campsite with a small stream cutting through it. This is created from a spring on the hillside.

Head out again approximately one mile where you reach the saddle and the beloved Teton view. The Wedge is the mountain on the right. Scramble carefully to the summit about another half mile or so (there is no trail but the summit is marked by a rock cairn). Alternatively, you can just find a nice spot to soak in the sun, the views, or energy from an impending storm.

<u>Miles</u> (roundtrip): approx. 7.8
<u>Elevation Gain</u>: approx. 3290 feet

Human Rating

- long drive, but solitude
- beautiful views
- easy access

Canine Rating

- plenty of water

Your dog's eye has many rods, which allow him to see better in low levels of light.

Peaked Mountain

Getting There: Head west on Highway 22 and drive through Wilson and over Teton Pass. Drive Highway 33 from Victor north 8 miles to Driggs. Turn right in downtown Driggs on Ski Hill Road toward Grand Targhee Ski Area. 11 miles further, reach the Ski Area and you can park in the lot.

The Hike: This well defined trail marked "Bike Loop C" starts at the base of Grand Targhee ski area and skirts the ski area boundary. The trail crosses Mill Creek at 0.9 miles (Mill Creek is dry by midsummer.) This is the canyon that divides Fred's Mountain and Peaked Mountain. Follow the trail as it heads right and around the base of Peaked. You will make a series of left turns as you traverse up the right side (south slope) of Peaked Mountain. Stay straight when a trail on the right leads down to Teton Canyon. At just about the summit, the well defined trail disappears. Stop here for a break, enjoying the breathtaking views of the Tetons and Treasure Mountain directly across the wide Teton Canyon.

From here, scramble up to the left side to reach the summit. Until you reach the summit, you will see groups of trees sprinkled along the mountain. The summit, marked by a cairn, is approximately half a mile from the trail ending. The summit of Peaked Mountain divides Grand Targhee ski area and Teton Canyon. Mary's Nipple is straight ahead. Fred's Mountain can be seen north of you, marked by the lift towers. Be sure to have your dog pack in water for himself because there is none to be found by midsummer.

To continue the loop for this hike, descend a somewhat hairy scramble to the saddle of Peaked and Mary's Nipple. Continue on the well defined trail down Fred's Mountain and onto the ski area service road.

Miles (roundtrip): approx. 5
Elevation Gain: approx. 1867 feet

Human Rating

- amazing views
- long drive
- short hike but easy access
- rock slides possible

Canine Rating 🦴🦴

- a trickle of water

Pinnacle Trail

Getting There: Driving west on Highway 22 through Wilson, go over Teton Pass into Victor. Drive 3.2 miles on Highway 33 north from downtown Victor toward Driggs. Turn right on signed Fox Creek Road 500S. Drive approximately 3.5 miles heading into Fox Creek Canyon. The quarry road is off limits to unauthorized vehicles. Stay right and park at the well signed trailhead parking lot.

The Hike: When you see the brown trail sign and the footbridge leading to a Forest Service sign for Fox Creek Pass, look to your left. Behind the piles of limestone there is an obvious road that heads up the opposite side of the Fox Creek Pass trail, which is on your right. A quarry is operational so you might see a trailer and equipment located at the beginning of the trail. Cut carefully behind the quarry equipment and you will soon discover the road. Head up and immediately after the first turn, look for the mildly worn trail heading along the left of the road. You soon realize that the trail simply parallels the road, higher up. After a short time, you pass an old sign from earlier blasting days in the quarry. The trail is apparent most of the way, being well defined. The trail crosses a small flowered meadow. Keep your eyes open for a series of rock cairns leading you across the meadow where the trail becomes well defined. As you head up the trail, wonderful views of 10,537-foot Housetop Mountain come into view. After a brief level section, the trail divides, giving you two options.

The right trail leads steeply up to an obvious ridge, passing interesting rock formations. The ridge is about 2 miles and 1300 feet above the trailhead. This is a nice half-day hike.

The left trail at the divide heads north and away from the canyon, cutting through meadows and young aspen groves. This route leads to an obvious saddle approximately 2280 feet above the trailhead. It makes a nice day hike.

Miles (roundtrip): approx. 4 - 6
Elevation Gain : approx. 1300-2280 feet

Human Rating	Canine Rating
• beautiful views	• water at the start
• solitude and wildlife	

West of Teton Pass (Hiking south from Victor and Driggs — Snake River Range)

The Snake River range is located south and southwest of Jackson, and south of Teton Valley on the western side of Teton Pass.

Hikes covered in the Snake River Range:

- Oliver Peak

- Pole Canyon

- Spencer Peak

Your dog's eye does have cones so he can see colors. However, colors are not as important for your dog as is movement.

Oliver Peak

Getting There: The trailhead is located on the west side of Teton Pass. From Jackson, drive west on Broadway and turn right onto Highway 22 at the "Y." Continue west on Highway 22 through Wilson; drive up and over Teton Pass. Near the base, turn left into the well marked Mike Harris Campground. The Campground is 11.9 miles after the Stagecoach in Wilson. Turn into the campground; cross the bridge and turn left onto a dirt road signed "Mike Harris Trail." Park there before the ruts in the road become too deep and proceed on foot.

The Hike: This is a decent workout up the Mike Harris Trail to the top of the ridgeline that connects Victor to Teton Pass. In early July, there is usually a bit of snow left. You can summit and return in approximately 4 hours, so this makes for a nice day hike and the wildflowers abound throughout the summer. Be thoughtful of your dog at the beginning and end of the hike by scrambling over to the creek and letting him have a quick dip.

Approximately half a mile from the parking area, the dirt road divides. Walk the right branch of the road. It soon narrows into the trail and stays distinct until the junction at the saddle.

To reach Oliver Peak stay left at this junction and proceed to the summit marked by a cairn. The Mike Harris trail can be combined with the Pole Canyon trail, making for a nice loop hike if you have shuttled a car. Be sure to bring a topo map.

Miles (roundtrip): approx. 8
Elevation Gain: approx. 2324 feet

Human Rating	Canine Rating 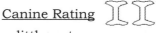
• beautiful hike	• little water
• beautiful wildflowers	• snow until
• solitude	midsummer
• can combine with Pole Canyon for a nice loop hike if you have shuttled a car or arranged for a pick up	

Pole Canyon

Getting There: From Jackson, drive west on Broadway, making a right turn onto Highway 22 at the "Y." Continue west on Highway 22 through Wilson and over Teton Pass to Highway 33 in downtown Victor. Turn left on Highway 31 toward Swan Valley. Approximately a half-mile further, turn left at the brown sign leading to Pole Canyon. Take a left immediately after entering the Forest Service land on Road 547 after a cattle guard that marks the national forest boundary. A short distance further, you will reach the trailhead parking lot. Around the lot, notice the remains of an old quarry site.

The Hike: Look for the log bridge and do some exploring before or after your hike. The trail follows the creek, which is a fast-moving river in spots. You cross it six times before heading up the canyon to the left. Although raging in early spring, it is a mere trickle by the end of summer.
After six creek crossings at a huge fallen tree, the trail turns sharply left and heads away from the creek, switchbacking three times before climbing through the heavily forested north-facing slope. Hiking up the ridgeline brings the Grand Teton into view to your right. Because the trail crosses the creek so many times, you might experience some difficulties crossing it in a storm, especially in the spring when the creek is raging.
Pole Canyon is the gatherer mecca. From common morels to red raspberries, this hike yields food most of the summer. Along the creek, there are many wonderful opportunities to gather the wonderful fruits that come only from your labor to get there. Even if you hike only as far the length of the river, be sure to bring your identification guides before eating anything you pick.

Miles (roundtrip): approx. 6
Elevation Gain: approx. 1750 feet

Human Rating

- a good workout
- can do a loop

Canine Rating

- plenty of water
- horses

Spencer Peak

<u>Getting There</u>: From Jackson, drive west on Broadway and turn right at the "Y" to Highway 22. Continue west on Highway 22 and drive through Wilson and over Teton Pass to Victor. Drive Highway 33 through Victor. Turn left onto Highway 31 toward Swan Valley. Set your odometer. Drive 6.6 miles further to the top of Pine Creek Pass. Turn left onto Rainey Creek Road. Continue on this pleasant road for 5.4 miles to the trailhead parking lot.

<u>The Hike</u>: Stunning views of the Big Holes await those who choose this relatively short hike. The western slope of the Teton Range spreads out to the northeast of you. The Snake River Range can be viewed to the south.

The hike begins after an information kiosk and a prominent brown sign. The trail is well defined in all but one section where evidence of horse and dirt bikes leads you to the rocky ridgeline of Spencer Peak. The trail is actually quite good until you get near the top of Spencer Peak and have to scramble up the rocky ridgeline on your right.

I have included this hike, in spite of the lack of water, because it is nice to hike with your dog without having to worry about grizzly bear encounters, and even nicer to exclude those in bear country altogether. There is very little bear activity in the Snake River Range but this does not mean that there are none. Be sure to pack some water for your dog, or let him carry it himself in a doggie backpack.

<u>Miles</u> (roundtrip): approx. 5.6
<u>Elevation Gain:</u> approx. 1570 feet

<u>Human Rating</u>

- beautiful drive
- stunning views
- solitude

<u>Canine Rating</u>

- some bicyclists
- not much water
- horses

Your dog can smell a teaspoon of salt in 13 gallons of water, or a bone buried 2 feet deep in the dirt.

West of Teton Valley (Hiking west from Victor and Driggs — Big Hole Range)

The Big Hole Range is located to the west of the Teton Valley, on the other side of Teton Pass. It has many hikes for those wanting to hike on the west side of Teton County. The Big Hole Range is wonderful for solitude, little bear activity, and breathtaking views.

Because many cattle graze here, respect the Forest Service gates, closing them behind you. Your dog cannot chase the livestock.

Hikes covered in the Big Hole Range:

- Rocky Peak
- An Unnamed Peak, 7834 feet
- Grove Creek
- Patterson Creek
- Packsaddle Lake

Rocky Peak

Getting There: From Jackson, drive west on Broadway and turn at the "Y" onto Highway 22. Continue on Highway 22 through Wilson and over Teton Pass to Highway 33 in downtown Victor. Turn left on Highway 31 (toward Swan Valley). Set your odometer. At 3.5 miles take a right on the Forest Service 900S road (it is gravel) when Highway 31 turns left; drive for 0.6 miles. Forest Service Road 900S ends at the 450/950 junction. You want 950, which goes straight into the National Forest. At 0.1 mile further you will reach Little Lowell Lake. Almost a half mile further, there is a prominent trail on the left. This is the beginning of the hike to Rocky Peak. Park off to the side.

The Hike: Little Lowell Lake is stocked with huge fish, but permission from the residents is necessary if you want to fish. However, you can let your dog have a swim. At just a little less than half a mile past Little Lowell Lake there is a trail on the left, leading to Rocky Peak. The trail immediately crosses a small stream.

The trail heads extremely steeply up the ridgeline but the reward at the top is breathtaking. The trail levels out into a majestic mature aspen grove. Head through the grove until the trail splits into a well worn triangle. You can go down to the left and access a lower elevation peak in the southernmost Big Holes. This unnamed peak is 7188 on the Fourth of July Peak quadrangle topo map.

You can head to the right and continue up the ridgeline to a gate, closing it behind you. The trail quickly climbs from moderate to steep. The trail goes through an aspen grove and then through a mixture of fir and pine. After two small switchbacks, the trail divides once more. The left seems to head to the southern ridgeline. Go straight and after a steep to moderate climb, you will arrive at the obvious saddle. The trail heads to the right and to the top of a rocky summit.

Miles (roundtrip): approx. 2.2
Elevation Gain: approx. 1068 feet

Human Rating

• short hike
• views and solitude

Canine Rating

• water at start

An Unnamed Peak, 7834 feet

Getting There: Drive west from Jackson on Broadway and turn at the "Y" onto Highway 22. Continue on Highway 22 through Wilson and over Teton Pass to Victor. Follow the directions to Rocky Peak. Continue on Forest Service road 950. At 0.5 miles past Little Lowell Lake, enter the Forest Service gates. Park to the side and continue on foot to the Unnamed Peak, which I have named after my dog, "Chief Peak."

The Hike: Little Lowell Lake is a pleasant little pond lined by pretty aspen trees. Fishing is allowed only with permission from the residents, but stop here to let your dog take a quick swim because there is only a little water on the hike. The trail is a well defined path often frequented by bikes that have left it deeply rutted. The trail narrows after crossing the stream.

As opposed to the hike up Rocky Peak, which follows a trail on the left off the road, this hike starts on the Forest Service road and heads straight up the canyon. Wind your way along the trail that parallels the stream, crossing it one more time before heading moderately up the right side of the canyon. Near the top of the saddle, you enter a beautiful mature aspen grove, and walk through groves of Douglas fir so thick that it gets almost dark. Shortly after, the Tetons come into view on your right and you arrive at an obvious saddle. From here, the entire southernmost western slope of the Tetons comes into view. From Taylor Mountain to Fred's Mountain, the view offers peace.

At the saddle you have a few options. Heading left brings you back down to Rocky Peak. Head right to access "Chief Peak." The trail is faint at first but quickly becomes distinct as it steeply climbs to the summit marked by a rock cairn. A group of fir trees and a flat spot just before the summit give you a great view of the Teton River snaking its way up Teton Valley. The summit of unnamed 7834 yields amazing views of the central Big Holes, also. This hike makes a nice half-day outing.

Miles (roundtrip): approx. 4
Elevation Gain: approx. 1514 feet

Human Rating	Canine Rating 
• views and solitude	• water
• can be linked with Rocky Peak	• bicyclists
	• winter use

Grove Creek

Getting There: From Jackson, drive west on Broadway and turn right onto Highway 22 at the "Y." Continue on Highway 22 through Wilson and over Teton Pass. Drive Highway 33 through Victor. Just past "The Old Cheese Factory" on the mall, turn left onto Cedron Road. Set your odometer. At 3 miles the road bends right, then left, zagging its way through tributaries of the Teton River, and early 1900 homesteader land still farmed today. 1.2 miles further, turn left onto 775S (4.2 miles total from Cedron turnoff in Victor). 0.2 miles further turn right at Grove Creek trail. Corral Creek is marked by a brown sign. Approximately 0.2 miles further the road becomes deeply rutted. I recommend parking to the side and continuing on foot. The road parallels Grove Creek on its right. Continue on the road reaching a Forest Service gate approximately 1/4 mile further. If the gate is closed, be sure to close it behind you after you go through.

The Hike: The trail parallels the creek, providing water for your dog . Just after the Forest Service gate, a brown Forest Service sign on your right confirms that you have entered Targhee National Forest and the Big Hole Range.
The trail slowly gains elevation, opening to a view of one possible destination, an unnamed peak, at an elevation of 7548 straight ahead. This peak is marked on the Fourth of July Peak quadrangle topo. Continue straight when a pack trail crosses Grove Creek on your left. Shortly after, you cross Grove Creek. Stay left and walk straight up Grove Creek when a runoff appears on your right. This is formed by a spring further up and is dry by the winter. Follow the clear, wide trail upward to your destination. Some off trail scrambling might be necessary to summit 7548 on your right after you reach the saddle. The trail can be looped to access Unnamed (Chief) Peak (previous page) if you have transportation back to your car parked at Grove Creek trailhead.

Miles (roundtrip): approx. 4 (depends on how far you drive on the road)
Elevation Gain: approx. 1388 feet

Human Rating
- solitude and good views
- can combine with Unnamed Peak (Chief Peak)

Canine Rating
- plenty of water
- winter use

Patterson Creek (and Red Mountain)

Getting There: From Jackson, drive west on Broadway and turn right at the "Y" onto Highway 22. Continue west on Highway 22 through Wilson and over Teton Pass. Drive Highway 33 through Victor. Just past "The Old Cheese Factory" on the mall, turn left onto Cedron Road. Set your odometer and at 5 miles further turn left onto 675 South. Disregard the "Dead End" sign and proceed slowly so as to give the residents their much-deserved peace. Park 1 mile further (6 miles total from the turnoff in Victor). There are privacy signs, reminding you how close you are to private land. Proceed through the Forest Service gate on foot, making sure to close it behind you.

The Hike: The trail weaves up the canyon, forcing you to navigate and jump over Patterson Creek countless times. It proceeds up the canyon mainly on the left side to a pronounced saddle on Mahogany Ridge. The summit of Red Mountain can also be reached via the Patterson Creek trail. This adds mileage. It is 10.4 miles roundtrip if you choose to add this wonderful mountain to your hike. Named for its distinctive red soil, Red Mountain is a prominent feature of the Big Hole Range.
Road 675 South becomes unsafe in winter months because it is not plowed in the winter. Because this forces anyone who wants to snowshoe or skin the trail to park precariously close to private land, it is not recommended in the winter.

Miles (roundtrip): approx. 7.2 to the saddle (7620 feet)
Elevation Gain: approx. 1460 feet

Human Rating

- beautiful views
- moderately steep
- good workout

Canine Rating

- water
- not recommended in winter

Packsaddle Lake

Getting There: From Jackson, drive west on Broadway and turn right at the "Y" onto Highway 22. Continue west on Highway 22 through Wilson and over Teton Pass. On Highway 33, drive through Victor and Driggs. 4 miles further north from the Driggs downtown intersection, turn left on Packsaddle Creek Road marked by a brown sign. Set your odometer. Continue straight, crossing the beautiful Teton River 5 miles further. At 8.4 miles from Highway 33, continue straight up the steep road. At 9.2 miles, continue straight over the cattle guard. At 10.4 miles, park at the signed junction next to some dilapidated corrals. Four-wheel drive is required.

The Hike: The hike starts at the corrals. Walk on the deeply rutted road, which is regraded in midsummer. After it is graded, you can drive this road but it gets dry and dusty. It is also a popular road for people to drive their 4-wheelers.

Go through a mixed forest for about a half mile when you leave private land and enter Targhee National Forest. This is marked by a cattle guard and a fence line with a small Forest Service sign.

The road/trail then bends southwest and heads toward Packsaddle Lake. Soon the trail levels and enters a grassy meadow. Disregard any faint trails and stay on the obvious main trail. Enter a lodgepole forest and start the moderate climb to the ridge above Packsaddle Lake. Eventually, the trail opens up to an old campsite used now as a parking area for those who 4-wheel drive to the lake. Packsaddle Lake is 800 feet below the parking area or flat spot. Follow the water runoff path. It is steep so be careful to watch your step. The lake is reached shortly after the steep descent.

There are some obvious old campsites on the lake, as well as a rope swing and diving board constructed of a downed lodgepole. There is fair fishing for anglers. Your dog will be well rewarded after a dusty hike by swimming for hours in the beautiful alpine lake. Retrace your steps back to the car.

Miles (roundtrip): approx. 4.8
Elevation Gain: approx. 800 feet

Human Rating

- long drive but good views
- a short, beautiful hike
  to a great lake

Canine Rating

- swimming at the lake
- 4-wheel-drive vehicles

The Saddle Horn Activity Center
(The Jackson Hole Nordic Center)
WINTER only

Getting There: From downtown Jackson, drive west on Broadway Avenue and turn right onto Highway 22 at the "Y." Drive west on Highway 22 and after crossing the Snake River, turn right onto Highway 390 to Teton Village. Turn left and park at the Ranch parking lot when you are at the Village.

The Hike: This is not a hike but a 6-kilometer Dog Loop on which you and your dog can get your exercise for the day. While you cross-country ski, your dog can run alongside you. And it is just perfect if you are one of those alpine skiers who leave your dog in your car all day — you won't have to feel guilty if you let your dog join you on this trail after you are through downhill skiing.

The trail is groomed daily. In addition to providing a good surface for your skiing, it means that you are responsible for using the Mutt Mitts to clean your dog's poop so that the trail can continue to be used by other dog owners.

The trail is open from 8:30 am to 4:30 pm during the ski season. This flat trail is located south of the Ranch parking lot at the base of the Jackson Hole Ski Resort.

Daily passes cost $8 and a season ticket is $125. You can use the same pass to ski on the 17-km "human-only" tracks without your dog.

For further information, call the Activity Center at (307) 739-2629.

Miles: 6 kilometers (just a little more than 3 miles)
Elevation Gain: none

Human Rating
- beautiful views
- groomed trails for you and your dog

Canine Rating
- no water but plenty of snow

Sharing the trail on the Snow King trail

Many dogs enjoy the Cache Creek hike

Ditch Creek water dogs

Ditch Creek playing dogs

Slide Lake

Greetings on the levee

Checking him out

"Who are you?"

Fetching a stick on the pond along the levee

River play along the levee

Wildflowers and dogs on the Old Pass

Crater Lake dogs

Ski Lake dogs

Dogs on a stick

Water stop along Coal Creek trail

"Chief" on Taylor Mountain

13   Directory of Dog Services

Animal Shelters

Jackson/Teton County Animal Shelter
3150 Adams Canyon Road
Jackson
(307) 733-2139

Teton Valley Humane Society (TVHS)
185 East 25 North
Driggs Idaho 83422
(208) 354-3499
humanesociety@pdt.net
http://www.pdt.net/tvhs

Apartments

Pioneer Homestead Apartments
Homes for the elderly and disabled
Dogs must be leashed when outside the apartment
830 East Hansen
Jackson
(307) 733-9787

Bed & Breakfasts

(some restrictions — check first)

Bentwood Bed & Breakfast
PO Box 561
4250 Raven Haven Road
Jackson
(307) 739-1411

Davy Jackson Inn
PO Box 20147
85 Perry Avenue
Jackson
(307) 739-2294

Don't Fence Me Inn
2350 North Moose-Wilson Road
Jackson
(307) 733-7979

Sassy Moose Inn
3895 North Moose-Wilson Road
Jackson
(307) 733-1277

Boarding, Kennels and Doggie Daycare

Animal Care Clinic of Jackson
415 East Pearl Street
Jackson
(307) 733-5590

Bark & Bounce Spa
PO Box 262
Wilson
(307) 733-0632

Cache Creek Veterinary Clinic
5700 West Highway 22
Wilson
(307) 733-6707

Critter Camp
Jackson Hole Veterinary Clinic
2950 Big Trails Drive (in Rafter J)
Jackson
(307) 733-4279

Critter Sitter
PO Box 262
Wilson
(307) 733-1407

Geyser Creek
- Member, American Boarding Kennel Association
- Indoor and outdoor heated runs
- Agility course
- Pickup and delivery service
Norina Fields
151 Bald Mountain Road
PO Box 846
Dubois
(307) 455-2702

Hairball Hotel
Family style, no cages
Dogs have the run of their own apartment at all times
Nearly one acre of fenced running room
Three separate yards if they need their own space for awhile
$10.00/day; you supply chow
Russ and Deb Herman
44 Depot Way
Victor Idaho
(208) 787-9828/2806

Jackson Hole Iditarod
Indoor/outdoor runs
(opening summer 2000)
Frank Teasley
(307) 733-7388

Kindness Kennels
Teton Veterinary Clinic
1225 South Gregory Lane
Jackson
(307) 733-2633

Rocky Mountain Canine Training Center
- Doggie daycare
- Large exercise area
- Agility course
Kean Bailey
Professional Gun Dog Trainer
Oatsy von Gontard
Certified Master Trainer/Behaviorist
Lower Melody Ranch
Jackson
(307) 733-0153

Spring Creek Animal Hospital
1035 West Broadway Avenue
(across from McDonald's at The Y)
Jackson
(307) 733-1606

Trail Creek Pet Center
• 20 years experience
• Veterinarian recommended
• Indoor and outdoor runs
• Large exercise area
• Special needs and special care dogs are welcomed
Pam Boyer
180 South 150 East
Driggs Idaho
(208) 354-2571

Campgrounds
(dogs must be leashed and poop must be scooped)

Flagg Ranch
PO Box 187
Located Between Grand Teton and Yellowstone National Parks
Highway 89 at the South Entrance to Yellowstone Park
Moran
(307) 543-2861
(800) 443-2311

Grand Teton National Park
Moose 83012
(307) 739-3603

Grand Teton Park KOA Campground
17750 East Highway 287
Moran
(307) 543-2483

Lazy J Corral
10755 South Highway 89
Hoback
(307) 733-1554

Lone Eagle Resort
PO Box 45
South of Jackson
Jackson
(307) 733-1090
(800) 321-3800

Snake River Park KOA
9705 South Highway 89
10 miles south of Jackson
(307) 733-7078

Yellowstone National Park
Madison Junction Campground
(307) 344-7381

Canine Capers

Agility Dogs — Geyser Creek
Norina Fields
151 Bald Mountain Road
PO Box 846
Dubois
(307) 455-2702

Agility Dogs — Rocky Mountain Canine Training Center
Oatsy Von Gontard
Lower Melody Ranch
Jackson
(307) 733-0153

4-H Dogs
Teton County Extension Office
(307) 733-3087

Friends
Joyce Corcoran
Teton County PAL
St John's Living Center
625 East Broadway Avenue
Jackson
(307) 739-7461

Frisbee Dogs
Terrie Fair
Teton County/Jackson Parks and Recreation Department
Jackson
(307) 733-5056

Grand Teton Kennel Club
Sandy Strout
855 Ponderosa Drive
Jackson
(307) 733-7684

Jackson Hole Retriever Club
Ron Kiehn
Jackson
(307) 739-9431

Jackson Hole Ski Patrol Avalanche Rescue Dogs
Jake Elkins
Jackson
(307) 733-2292

PAWS of Jackson Hole
Judy Eddy
PO Box 13033
Jackson 83002
(307) 733-9167
PAWS@dog.com

Pet Fair
Judy Eddy
PO Box 11822
Jackson 83002
(307) 733-9167

Pet Partner® Teams
Judy Eddy
Teton County PAL
PO Box 10023
Jackson
(307) 733-9167

Show Dogs
Juanita McGhee
Jackson
(307) 733-2084

Sled Dogs
See listings under Tours, Sled Dog

Teton County PAL
Judy Eddy
PO Box 10023
Jackson
(307) 733-9167
tcpal@rmisp.com
http://www.dogsaver.org/tetoncountypal

Wyoming K-9 Search and Rescue
Janet Wilts
PO Box 136
Moose
(307) 734-9052

Condominiums

Jackson Hole Lodge
(small dogs only)
PO Box 1805
420 West Broadway Avenue
Jackson
(307) 733-2992

Snow King Resort
PO Box SKI
400 East Snow King Avenue
Four Blocks from the Town Square
Jackson
(307) 733-5200
(800) 522-KING

Cross-Country Ski Trail

The Saddle Horn Activity Center
(The Jackson Hole Nordic Center)
Teton Village
(307) 739-2629

Dining

Many books similar to this for other areas of the country include restaurants where your dog can lie at your feet on outdoor decks. However, Wyoming state law forbids animals on any restaurant premises, including outdoor areas. Basically, dogs are not allowed where food is prepared or served. The reasoning behind the law is that dogs can transmit tapeworms, many people do not like to have dogs around them when they are eating, some dogs get into fights, and some dogs might not be confined on leash but are allowed to wander through the eating area. So, do not look for restaurants in Teton County (or anywhere in Wyoming) that will let your dog join you while you dine outside at a restaurant.

Grooming

All About Pets
Mobile pet-grooming business
Your home or business
Julie Johnson
(307) 733-5222

Critter Clipper
Jackson Hole Veterinary Clinic
2950 Big Trails Drive (in Rafter J)
Jackson
(307) 733-4279

Cyndi's Pet Grooming
Teton Veterinary Clinic
1225 South Gregory Lane
Jackson
(307) 734-2853

<u>Geyser Creek</u>
• Grooming
• Pickup and Delivery
Norina Fields
151 Bald Mountain Road
PO Box 846
Dubois
(307) 455-2702

<u>Spring Creek Animal Hospital</u>
1035 West Broadway Avenue
(across from McDonald's at The Y)
Jackson
(307) 733-1606

<u>Trail Creek Pet Center</u>
Pam Boyer
180 South 150 East
Driggs Idaho
(208) 354-2571

Guest Ranches

<u>Mad Dog Guest Ranch</u>
Teton Village Road
Jackson
(307) 733-3729

<u>Turpin Meadow Ranch</u>
(restrictions)
East End of Buffalo Valley Road
Moran
(307) 543-2496
(800) 743-2496

Hotels (see Motels)

Kennels (see Boarding)

Lodging
See type of lodging units

Motels and Hotels

Alpine Motel
70 South Jean
Jackson
(307) 739-3200

Antler Inn
PO Box 575
43 West Pearl Avenue
One block west of the Town Square
Jackson
(307) 733-2535
(800) 522-2406

Cache Creek Motel
PO Box 918
390 North Glenwood Street
Three blocks from the Town Square
Jackson
(307) 733-7781
(800) 843-4788

Camp Creek Inn
12330 South Highway 191
Hoback
(307) 733-3099

Colter Bay Village Cabins
Highway 89
10 miles north of Moran
Grand Teton National Park
(307) 543-2811 (same day reservations)
(307) 543-3100 (future reservations)

Cottages at Snow King
PO Box 1053
470 King Street
Four blocks from the Town Square
Jackson
(307) 733-3480

Crystal Springs Inn
32985 West McCollister Drive
Teton Village
(307) 733-4423

Davy Jackson Inn
PO Box 20147
85 Perry Avenue
Jackson
(307) 739-2294

Elk Country Inn
PO Box 1255
480 West Pearl Avenue
4-1/2 blocks from the Town Square
Jackson
(307) 733-2364
(800) 483-8667

Flat Creek Motel
PO Box 20013
1935 North Highway 26 & 89
One block north of the Town Square
Jackson
(307) 733-5276
(800) 438-9338

49'er Inn & Suites
PO Box 1948
330 West Pearl Avenue
Four blocks to the Town Square
Jackson
(307) 733-7550
(800) 451-2980

Hatchet Motel
19980 East Highway 287
Moran
(307) 543-2413

Hillside Motel
945 West Broadway Avenue
Jackson
(307) 733-3391

Jackson Hole Lodge
PO Box 1805
420 West Broadway Avenue
Jackson
(307) 733-2992

Jackson Lake Lodge
(cottages only)
Highway 89
5 miles north of Moran
Grand Teton National Park
(307) 543-2811 (same day reservations)
(307) 543-3100 (future reservations)

Motel 6
(small dogs only)
1370 West Broadway Avenue
Jackson
(307) 733-1620

Old West Cabins
5750 South Highway 89
6 miles south of Jackson
Jackson
(307) 733-0333

Painted Buffalo Inn
PO Box 2547
400 West Broadway Avenue
Three blocks to the Town Square
Jackson
(307) 733-4340
(307) 288-3866

Prospector Motel
PO Box 494
155 North Jackson
Jackson
(307) 733-4858

Signal Mountain Lodge
PO Box 50
Grand Teton National Park
Moran
(307) 543-2831

Snow King Resort
PO Box SKI
400 East Snow King Avenue
Four blocks from the Town Square
Jackson
(307) 733-5200
(800) 522-KING

Split Creek Ranch
North of Jackson
(307) 733-7522

Teton Gables Motel
1140 West Highway 22
Jackson
(307) 733-3723

Wolf Moon Inn
PO Box 917
285 North Cache
Two blocks from the Town Square
Jackson
(307) 733-2287
(800) 964-2387

Wyoming Inn of Jackson
930 West Broadway Avenue
Jackson
(307) 734-0035

Property Management
(Occasionally, dog-friendly rentals are available)

Alpine Vacation Rentals and Management
PO Box 387
Teton Village Road
Teton Village
(307) 734-1161
(800) 876-3968

Black Diamond Vacation Rentals & Real Estate
PO Box 2297
290 East Broadway Avenue
Jackson
(307) 733-6170

Circle C Property Management
PO Box 3730
Jackson
(307) 733-4337

Ely & Associates Property Management
PO Box 1001
180 North Center Street
Jackson
(307) 733-8604
(800) 735-8310

First Cabin Property Management
1230 Ida Drive
Wilson
(307) 739-9145

Grand Teton Property Management
PO Box 2282
270 Veronica Lane
Jackson
(307) 733-0205
(800) 903-6946

Hoffman & Associates
480 South Cache Street
Jackson
(307) 733-3436
(800) 735-8385

M&S Consulting
PO Box 4338
1055 Gregory Lane
Jackson
(307) 733-5881

Mountain Property Management
PO Box 2228
175 South King Street
Jackson
(307) 733-1684
(800) 992-9948

Prime Properties of Jackson Hole
1230 North Ida Lane
Wilson
(307) 739-9145
(800) 989-9145

Rancho Deluxe Realty
125 South King Street
Jackson
(307) 733-9111

Rendezvous Mountain Rentals & Property Management
PO Box 11338
Jackson
(307) 739-9050
(888) 739-2565

Resorts

Antler Inn
PO Box 575
43 West Pearl Avenue
One block west of the Town Square
Jackson
(307) 733-2535
(800) 522-2406

Flagg Ranch
PO Box 187
Located between Grand Teton and Yellowstone National Parks
Highway 89 at the South Entrance to Yellowstone Park
Moran
(307) 543-2861
(800) 443-2311

49'er Inn & Suites
PO Box 1948
330 West Pearl Avenue
Four blocks to the Town Square
Jackson
(307) 733-7550
(800) 451-2980

Signal Mountain Lodge
PO Box 50
Grand Teton National Park
Moran
(307) 543-2831

Snow King Resort
PO Box SKI
400 East Snow King Avenue
Four blocks from the Town Square
Jackson
(307) 733-5200
(800) 522-KING

Sitting, Dog (in your home)

Alpha Animal Care
• Pet sitting and walking
• Specializes in pet massage
• All species
• Insured and bonded
(307) 733-5352

<u>Pet Partners</u>

We'll make it fun for your pets!
- Feeding rituals
- Exercise
- Special needs

Jackson

(307) 733-0705

<u>Heather C Young</u>

• Local and international references
• Available for house sitting
• Expertise in many different areas of pet care, including exotic animals
• Experience as third-level zookeeper
• Vet technician
• Exclusive training in falconry
• Big Apple Circus assistant horse trainer

(307) 734-7093

(307) 690-7093

Sled Dog Tours

Continental Divide Sled Dogs Inc.
Daily by reservation only
Half day, full day or overnight trips to Brooks Lake Lodge. Full
  day or half-day to yurt. Three-day backcountry trips, with
  one night in a backcountry cabin and one night in a yurt.
  Meals, transportation and clothing are provided.
PO Box 84
Dubois
(307) 739-0165
(307) 455-3052
(800) 531-MUSH (6874)

Dog Tours by Washakie Outfitting
Half day, full day and overnight trips. Half day snowmobile
  and half day dog sled combo trip. Meals, clothing, and
  transportation from the Jackson area provided.
Billy and Jackie Snodgrass
1658 Horse Creek Road
Dubois
(307) 733-3602

Jackson Hole Iditarod Sled Dog Tours
Learn mushing firsthand as you drive your own sled team
Jackson-based tours in the Bridger Teton National Forest
Daily by reservation only
Half day, 10- to 12-mile tour. A full-day 20-mile trip lets you
  soak in a natural 105° hot spring on the famous Granite Creek
  Canyon tour. Meals, transportation, and supplemental cloth-
  ing are provided.
PO Box 1940
11 Granite Creek Road
Jackson
(307) 733-7388

Moon Mountain Ranch Dog Sled Tours

Dog sled rides lasting 2-1/2 hours wind through Rick's Basin area. Food and beverages are included. BBQ cookout includes 3-1/2 hour tour. Moonlight tour also available. $100 to $175 for adults; $40 to $70 for children. Free transportation is provided from Jackson Hole.

Grand Targhee Resort
June Davies
(208) 354-2845
(800) Targhee (827-4433)

Supplies

Albertson's

• Assortment of dry and canned foods
• Dog treats and Dog toys
• Dog collars and Dog leashes
• More

West Broadway Avenue
Jackson
(307) 733-5950

Animal Care Clinic of Jackson

• Science Diet
• Natural Life Pet Products
• Dog collars
• Nail clippers

415 East Pearl Street
Jackson
(307) 733-5590

Big Dog Sportwear

• Dog leashes and collars
• Dog fashion clothing (coats, sweaters)

80 East Broadway Avenue
Jackson
(307) 734-2886

Bitterroot Trading Company

• Pepper Spray

170 West Broadway Avenue
Jackson
(307) 733-4192

Driggs Veterinary Clinic
• Science Diet
129 North Highway 33
Driggs Idaho
(208) 354-2212

Food Town
• Dry and canned foods
• Dog treats and Dog toys
• Flea and tick collars
• Dog shampoos and Dog brushes
• More
970 West Broadway Avenue
Jackson
(307) 733-0450

Harvest Natural Foods
• Natural Life Pet Products
130 West Broadway Avenue
Jackson
(307) 733-5418

Herb Store, The
• Vita-Mineral Mix
• Dream Coat
• Natural Herbal Ear Wash
• Derma Dream Natural Healing Salve
• More
170 East Deloney Avenue
Jackson
(307) 733-4142

Hungry Jack's
• Natural Life Pet Products
• Dry and canned foods
• More
5655 West Highway 22
Wilson
(307) 733-3561

Invisible Fence of Wyoming

- Invisible Fencing brand pet containment and in-home pet management system (the ONLY system awarded the ASPCA Seal of Approval and the Consumer Digest Best Buy Award). Keeping Jackson Hole's pets safely at home where they belong since 1987. Lifetime warranties and a one-year money-back containment guarantee
- Plexidoor pet doors
- Wild Bill's squirrel-proof bird feeders
- "Fooey" (14 times more bitter than Bitter Apple)
- Full Invisible Fence training and obedience training
- Plenty of free advice
- Breeders of the extremely rare and gentle Native American Chinook dog. We welcome you to visit Winterset Farm Pure-bred Chinook Kennels.
- Please call for a free estimate.

TJ and Grace Anderson
(307) 733-DOGS
(800) 210-5234
http://www.ifco.com

Jackson Hole Book Trader

- selection of used books about dogs

970 West Broadway Avenue, Suite F
Jackson
(307) 734-6001
http://www.onvillage.com/@/jacksonbook

Jackson Hole Resort Store

- Dog booties
- Dog feeding dishes
- Dog treats
- Dog feeding placemats
- Automobile harnesses
- More

50 North Center Street
Jackson
(307) 739-2767
email: tramdock@jacksonhole.com
http://www.jacksonhole.com/ski/store.tmpl

Jackson Hole Veterinary Clinic
• Science Diet
• Eukanuba
• Natural Life Pet Products
• Dog dental and skin care products
• Dog shampoos for allergy relief
2950 Big Trails Drive (in Rafter J)
Jackson
(307) 733-4279

KMart
• Dry food and canned food
• Dog treats and Dog toys
• Dog collars
• Dog beds and Dog crates
• More
1357 South Highway 89
Jackson
(307) 739-0865

Orvis
• Dog beds
• Dog collars and Dog leashes
• Dog chew toys
• Dog bowls and Dog biscuits
• Various dog-related and themed gift items
485 West Broadway Avenue
Jackson
(307) 733-5407

Park Place Market & Deli
• Dry and canned foods
545 North Cache
Jackson
(307) 733-7926

Paws of Jackson Hole
• Canine Visor Caps
PO Box 13033
Jackson
(307) 733-9167

Pet Security Plus
Eric Weber
• Hidden Dog Fence
• Dog no-bark collars
• Remote trainers
With the safe, effective Pet Alert™ Containment System, it'll keep
   your dog at home.
To get your paws on Pet Alert, call
(307) 739-9544
(307) 690-0128

Sacred Hawk
• Natural Life Pet Products
• Dr Goldstein's Health Nuggets for Dogs
• Tasha's Herbs
6680 Lupine Trail
PO Box 316
Wilson
(307) 739-8519

Skinny Skis
• Dog backpacks
• Dog booties
• Dog collapsible bowls
• Pepper spray
• More
65 West Deloney
Jackson
(307) 733-6094

Spike Camp Sports
• Pepper spray
355 North Cache Street
Jackson
(307) 733-4406

Spring Creek Animal Hospital
- Nature's Recipe
- Science Diet
- C.E.T. chews and Pet-Tabs
- Nature's Miracle Products (skunk odor remover)
- Nail clippers
- Dog combs and rakes
- Rawhide
- Dog booties

1035 West Broadway Avenue
Jackson
(307) 733-1606

Tasha's Herbs for Dogs and Cats
- 24 liquid herbal formulas for wellness and herbal treatments

1200 South Gregory Lane
Jackson
(307) 734-0142

Teton Bookshop
- Limited selection of books about hunting dogs

25 South Glenwood Street
Jackson
(307) 733-9220

Teton County PAL
- Instant-make ID tags
- Safety alert notices

PO Box 10023
Jackson
(307) 733-9167

Teton Mountaineering
- Dog backpacks
- Pepper spray
- Dog leashes and Dog collars
- Packable food and water bowls

170 North Cache
Jackson
(307) 733-3595

Teton Veterinary Clinic
- Science Diet

1225 South Gregory Lane
Jackson
(307) 733-2633

Valley Book Store
- Complete Selection of books about dogs

125 North Cache Street (in Gaslight Alley)
Jackson
(307) 733-4533
http://www.onvillage.com/@/valleybooks
http://www.valleybook.com

Valley Feed & Pet Shoppe
- Eagle
- Iams
- Nature's Recipe
- NutraMax
- Science Diet
- Dog booties
- Dog harnesses and dog backpacks
- Dog hunting vests and fluorescent collars
- Dog collapsible bowls and no-spill water dishes
- Retrieving dummies and training aids
- Travel crates
- Herbal motion sickness medicines
- More

1175 South Highway 89
Jackson
(307) 733-5945

Westside Store & Deli
- Dry and canned foods
- Dog chew toys
- Dog flea collars

4015 West Lake Creek Drive
In the Aspens
Wilson
(307) 733-6202

Wilson Hardware & Lumber
• NutraMax
• Big Red
• Dog choke collars
• Leather leashes
1275 North West Street
Wilson
(307) 733-9664

Training, Obedience

Ain't Misbehavin'
Hanna Cohan
PO Box 10544
Jackson
(307) 734-0626

Blackwater Labradors
• Training
• Problem solving
• Alternative methods
• Local references
Johanne Fleming
(208) 787-2802

Dog Sense
"Build a happier and more rewarding relationship with your
    dog"
• Obedience training
• Behavior problems
• Puppy training
• 2-day seminars
Kathy Greger and Chris Hamer
(307) 733-3608

Grand Teton Kennel Club
"Grand Teton Kennel Club teaches you to train your dog"
• Basic and advanced obedience classes
• Reduced rates for animals adopted from the Animal Shelter
• Special puppy classes
• Group and private lessons
• Sponsor of Teton County Fair Dog Show
Barbara (307) 733-7747 (days)
Sandy Strout (307) 733-7684 (evenings)

Invisible Fence of Wyoming
• Full training for your pet to the Invisible Fence system
• Obedience training
TJ and Grace Anderson
(307) 733-DOGS
(800) 210-5234
http://www.ifco.com

On Command! Dog Training and Animal Management
"A Well Trained Dog is a Happy Dog"
Private lessons for
• Obedience training
• Service Dog training
• Way of Life training
• Behavioral modification
• Soft-mouth retrieval
• Invisible Fence training
Sarah Harrison
PO Box 13514
Jackson
(307) 734-0720

Roche Jaune All-Breed Dog Training
Who's Training Who?
• Basic obedience
• Advanced obedience
• Problem solving
• Located on 40 acres
• Veterinarian recommended
• Training in the Valley for 13 years
• German Shepherd breeder
Jill Straley - Trainer
138 Fremont Lake Road
Pinedale
(307) 367-2687

Rocky Mountain Canine Training Center
Kean Bailey
Professional Gun Dog Trainer
Oatsy Von Gontard
Certified Master Trainer/Behaviorist
• Obedience
  (private and resident programs)
• Gun dogs
• Assistance dogs
• Puppy preschool and socialization class
• Behavior problem solving
• Agility
Lower Melody Ranch
Jackson
(307) 733-0153

Trail Creek Pet Center
David P'Pool Obedience Classes
(summer only)
•10-week course
• Beginner and advanced
• Problem solving
• Regulation training
Pamela Boyer
(208) 354-2571

Vacation Rentals

Alpine Vacation Rentals and Management
PO Box 387
Teton Village Road
Teton Village 83025
(307) 734-1161
(800) 876-3968

Black Diamond Vacation Rentals & Real Estate
PO Box 2297
290 East Broadway Avenue
Jackson
(307) 733-6170

Veterinarians

Animal Care Clinic of Jackson
Carolyn Gunn DVM
Ernie Patterson DVM
Erica Periman DVM
• Companion animals
• Horses
• Ranch calls
415 East Pearl Street
Jackson
(307) 733-5590

Cache Creek Veterinary Clinic
Wendy Webb DVM
• Companion animals
• Small animals & equine
• IVAS certified veterinary acupuncture
5700 West Highway 22
Wilson
(307) 733-6707

Driggs Veterinary Clinic
Donald J Betts DVM
John C Bigley DVM
Large and small animals
Surgery, Medicine and Reproduction
129 North Highway 33
Driggs Idaho
(208) 354-2212

Jackson Hole Veterinary Clinic
Tim Gwilliam DVM
Jack Konitz DVM
Kaley Parent DVM
• Caring for all species
• Large & small animal orthopedics & surgery
• 24-hour emergency service
2950 Big Trails Drive (in Rafter J)
Jackson
(307) 733-4279

Mariposa Mobile Veterinary Service
Marybeth Minter DVM
• Providing home veterinary care for your dog & cat
• Integrating holistic principles in veterinary practice
• House calls
• Acupuncture
Kelly
(307) 734-6070

Spring Creek Animal Hospital
Dan Forman DVM
MJ LaRue Forman DVM (Board Certified Internal Medicine)
Katherin Luderer DVM
• Specializing in dogs, cats, birds & exotic species
• Board Certified Dermatologist & Orthopedic Surgeon
• Soft-tissue surgery
• 24-hour emergency service
1035 West Broadway Avenue
Jackson
(307) 733-1606

Teton Veterinary Clinic
Al Barton DVM
Michael Dennis DVM
Ken Griggs DVM
• All species
• Oldest practice in Jackson Hole (Established 1969)
• Endoscopic examinations
• Ultrasound
• 24-hour emergency service
1225 South Gregory Lane
Jackson
(307) 733-2633

Victor Veterinary Hospital
Jane Linville-Wiens DVM
• Affiliated with Spring Creek Animal Hospital
• Mixed animal practice
• Ultrasound
• Medical and surgical services
255 South Agate Avenue
Victor Idaho
(208) 787-2114

14 Musings About Dogs

My Hunting Dogs

by Justin Adams

Some homeowner associations pay no heed to an old joke about words and phrases seldom heard in the South. I am thinking of "checkmate" and "we have enough dogs." I need a Labrador retriever and find myself legally restricted to the four dogs I already own, two retired English Springer spaniels to whom I am eternally devoted, one active-duty Springer, and a three-year-old English setter. One way to interpret the rules, which seems sensible to me, is to count my lovely retired Springers as fractional dogs, but my god fearing wife, Josephine, will not subscribe to this notion. If the old guys, who are awake only two to four hours each day counted as halves, then I would have an empty dog slot and could acquire a Lab. Josephine thinks our ancient Springer spaniels would find this calculation so demeaning that they might bite me if they knew about it.

The problem centers on long, cold water duck retrieves. I have never known a Springer who could keep up with a Labrador on long, cold swims. Consequently, hunting ducks without a Lab means hunting without my ten-gauge, thus restricting myself to the closer shots. As problems go, this is not terrible, and my active-duty Springer, "Sam Spaniel," and I manage the situation happily.

Early in the season through October, we hunt moraines around Teton County. Moraines are extensive rock piles studded with small potholes and aspen thickets. "Sam" sniffs along for grouse, covering every thicket thoroughly and with the greatest expectations, always staying close to me in the tradition of a flushing dog. This dog brings new meaning to the phrase, "making game," because he seems intent on inventing a bird for me to shoot if he cannot find one. And we do manage to shoot grouse, particularly on days when we work very hard. "Sam" and I figure that we walk at least three miles for every grouse in the bag. So it is a good thing that the ruffed grouse is among the best-tasting of all game birds. Otherwise, people might think that we are misdirected in our life's pursuit.

As we approach the occasional potholes formed by low places in the rocky moraines and beaver dams along the drainages, I order "Sam" to heel and we creep up to the water ready for action. Teal are abundant and we shoot these early migra-

153

tors first, saving the mallards for later in the season. Then, the mallard drake's plumage is more pronounced, allowing me to shoot males only and save the hens for the next nesting season. "Sam" has trouble with this program and complains loudly when I jump an early season flock of mallards where the drakes are indistinguishable from the hens but do not shoot. Even a well-loved dog can have tough times.

Snipe, the most neglected game bird in North America, are found along mud flats around beaver dams in Teton County. "Sam" takes great delight in retrieving these diminutive birds when I can hit the little darters. Three breasts make an entree and we bake them like mourning doves. With a limit of eight, we get a pretty good number of meals. Wyoming game law requires nontoxic shot for snipe hunting because they live in wetlands. One should take note that nontoxic shot is required for ducks as well and the kind of mixed bag grouse and duck hunting that "Sam" and I pursue in the moraines also demands nontoxic shot. This is especially important because Trumpeter swans spend lazy afternoons on some of the potholes. On several occasions, a family of swans has sputtered mud and spray on a surprised spaniel and me as they fly out of the small ponds where we had hoped to find teal.

"Lola," my three-year-old setter, does her early season hunting on the sage flats of neighboring Sublette County, looking for sage grouse. This is an arduous undertaking and the rewards are spotty at best. Nevertheless, "Lola" loves crashing through the sage and covers ground efficiently, regularly ranging out a quarter of a mile from me. When she locates the birds, she marks them for me with a staunch point and holds it until I arrive at the scene to flush the birds. Early in the season, we catch the grouse spread out and they rise a couple at a time, making it easy for me to shoot my limit of three. "Lola" appreciates the ziplock bag that I carry so I can share my drinking water with her since these hunts frequently involve long walks in the sun away from water.

These early season sage grouse hunts are training and conditioning for later trips to eastern Montana and western North Dakota, but also for ruffed grouse hunting in Teton County. "Lola"'s best opportunity to hunt our County is a window of time between the last of the leaves and the beginning of deep snow. Otherwise, in the tradition of a pointing dog, she ranges where I cannot see her and I find myself stumbling in circles when she is out of sight and locked on point. She sports a four-inch-wide blaze orange collar at this time of the year to help me locate her against the light snow background that has begun to accumulate. We try to hunt aspen thickets along logging roads and stay away from the moraines because the hiking across the rocks, glazed in ice and covered with light snow, becomes hazardous. I have several gashes on my gunstock that convince most hunter friends to leave their fancy guns at home at this time of year. The grouse are smarter and fly more aggressively, making the shooting sportier later in the season, even though the birds are easier to see without leaves on the trees.

As the winter progresses and the snow becomes too deep for grouse hunting on our steep mountainsides with "Lola," I return to duck hunting with "Sam Spaniel." We walk along the Snake River, hoping to jump some greenheads or catch a flight of goldeneyes coming down the channel. The halcyon days of watching "Sam" dive beneath the slime of a pothole on a balmy October day to retrieve a crippled teal have passed. I wear snowshoes and "Sam" springs along beside me, laboriously lunging through snow deep enough to cover him. The shots are longer and I frequently pass them. The problem is doubled barreled: crippling game that never make it to the kitchen and exposing "Sam" to the hazards of fast-flowing river water that could wash him into a snag. I need a Labrador to complement my ten-gauge that I want to use. This strategy would allow me so many shots that I now pass for fear of crippling ducks that "Sam" could not retrieve.

Our duck and grouse supply lasts halfway through the ski season. Josephine, a gourmet cook planning to write a wild game cookbook, conducts marvelous culinary experiments to my benefit. After dinner, the old guys lick the plates before we load the dishwasher. Then, we climb beneath our goosefeather comforter with our best buddies, who sniff by day and snuggle by night.

Dealing with Your Dog's Death

by Judy F. Eddy

Dogs have one major fault — their lives are too short. When they die, they leave a void in our hearts. However, there are also practical considerations — what do you do with your dead dog?

The Town Ordinances state that "when any dog has died, the remains of such dog shall be buried beneath the surface of the ground at the City dump or any other appropriate location. The remains shall not be placed in garbage cans for pickup and disposal."

Many people choose to bury their dog in their own yard. If this is not practical, they will have their dog cremated. How do you do the latter? Contact your veterinarian for help — he or she will be able to take care of this for you. One of the local veterinarian offices has a crematorium on its premises.

If you find a dead dog along the road, call the Animal Shelter (307-733-2139). The director will try to locate the dog's owner and she is always ready with hugs for those who learn of their dog's demise in this way.

It is sometimes necessary to have your veterinarian euthanize your dog, especially when your dog is in great pain. The decision is always difficult and is very stressful and filled with grief. You will know when the time has come; indications include a lack of appetite, inactivity or a glazed look. Typical euthanasia is an overdose of anesthesia that suppresses brain activity and stops the heart. Your dog will feel no pain and death occurs in less than a minute. In some cases, a physiologic reaction might occur (e.g., muscle movement) or your dog might not close his eyes when he dies. Do not be concerned; he did NOT suffer. Our veterinarians are very compassionate and understand your need to grieve.

Experts suggest that you should comfort your child(ren) and give them extra attention during the grieving process. Explain the pet's death in absolute terms rather than using euphemisms (e.g., "put to sleep").

To help you and/or your child(ren) cope, you can call Reverend Suzanne Harris (307-733-7702) who is a grief counselor. She will help ease your troubled decision. She will also be able to help you cope with the grief after your dog has died.

People grieve and recover in many ways. Following are stories from four valley residents. Perhaps their tales will help you when you face a similar tragedy.

"Oatmeal"

by Clare Payne Symmons

"Oatmeal" died on July 3 1999. She was only 18 months old. She died because she loved us too much.

We went fishing that beautiful day. We moved from our first location because Mike thought we were too close to the highway. "Oatmeal" ran between us, playing fetch as we came ashore to move downstream. She hated to be apart from us and even braved swimming in the river to be near us. There, she would tread against the current until she had to return to shore.

Eventually, I ended up on one side of the highway and Mike was on the other. I guess she went to say "hi" to Mike — all I heard was the thump as her young body hit the mobile home. We had lost our baby.

I remember the day Mike came home and told me that the shelter had two litters of puppies. We had talked about getting a dog but never had we visited the Animal Shelter. "Oatmeal" was a scared little pup when she entered our home. She learned fast — potty-trained that first week. At first, Mike had to lift her into the van to go to work with him. Later, you would ask her if she wanted to go to work and she would jump with pleasure. She loved us purely, trusted us completely. She was one of those dogs who could look in your eyes and speak volumes. I knew when she was hungry; I knew when she was scared. She knew everything about me.

When we drove home that day, I left a piece of myself by the banks of the river. We left her there, under a shady tree, within the sound of the water she loved so well. The next day, we mostly sat in shock. That evening, I took a walk — our walk. I saw her running ahead, looking back and telling me to hurry up. We went together to the stream where I threw in pebbles and she pulled out boulders. We went home together, listening to the sounds of the 4th of July concert.

On Monday, both Mike and I decided to go to work even though it was a holiday. Neither one of us could be in the house any more, as empty as it was. I am sure that before Mike climbed into his van, he called out to her to hurry up. She was with Mike every day — I always said she was his business partner. I can only imagine his pain and I ached for him as much as I ached for me.

By the end of the week, Mike checked with me on getting another dog. It was so very lonely for him, not having her by his side. No dog could ever replace her, but we could have a chance at giving another pup a good home, giving her love, and receiving love in return.

I started contacting the Animal Shelters and by the end of the next week, I had created a network that covered three states, with many people looking for the right puppy for us. That was when I learned I was not alone. There were others who loved their pets as deeply as we had loved "Oatmeal." I joined the "club" of the bereaved. I drew great comfort from the words and stories of others — the pictures and memorials, the caring calls from Shelter managers. I got two different versions of "The Rainbow Bridge" (see below).

Eventually we found "Pagan." Barely (probably forcibly) weaned, she had been left with her five littermates in the woods in Idaho. As we picked her up a few days later, the Shelter employee who had driven her from Pocatello to Idaho Falls said, "Thank you. The odds were against her. I know you will give her a good home."

What we learned from "Oatmeal" was that love is not finite. There is always room for more. The last day I took "our" walk, "Oatmeal" left me but with such an overwhelming feeling of gratitude and love that it really is okay. I built a little shrine of the rocks she pulled from the stream, and said goodbye. That night in my sleep, she came running full-tilt, a great huge grin on her face, right into my arms. I still miss her but she isn't really gone, and I thank her for all she gave us.

A Prayer: "Please let me be the person my dog thinks I am."

"Bear"

by JC Weinbrandt

And so, "Bear," as your life gently fades away from me I recall the past 9-1/2 years with you. As a black Labrador puppy you were my pick of the litter. I knew I wanted to train you as a working dog so on that magical 49th day — the day of imprinting — you came into our home, our lives and our hearts.

Search and Rescue was your passion. We played it with you as you grew up. You dug hundreds of my children's friends out of the snow with much gusto as they played "FIND" in our backyard. You were obsessed with counting heads when our family hiked together. You were proud and content when you knew we were all found.

Then you began your era of working and comforting strangers who were lost, injured, drowned or buried in avalanches. You knew the swift water well and showed me where there was scent. And, you also mourned the loss of lives. You displayed those amber eyes full of untold knowledge. You were drawn to the family members who were grieving. You sought them out and offered comfort with those amber eyes of understanding and compassion for their grief and worry. You mourned for days afterwards. At times my three children wondered if it was worth it — when you isolated yourself for a period of time to grieve the losses. But the children were always very proud to call you their friend and pet.

When the news came to me from Colorado State University Veterinary School that your cough was due to massive tumors in your lungs giving you only a few weeks to live, my grief was overwhelming. I tried so hard to hold back my tears in the waiting room but finally knew the other people would somehow understand and relate. I knew in my heart that I shall never have another "Bear ."

I relished the moments I had left with you. I held you at night and told you endless times how wonderful you were. And I feared — feared the day when I would say, "let's go "Bear"" and you, too weak and tired, wouldn't want to "go find." I knew this was my signal that you had truly given up and needed to rest in peace.

When that dreaded day came, my vet was compassionate and caring. She came to our home and sat with our family. We surrounded you with fresh lilacs, laid you on an Indian blanket and covered you with a royal purple polar fleece wrap. My stepdaughter snapped the last photo of you with me at your side. I still felt and saw the profound depth of your amber eyes — with the knowledge of a lifetime of victories, sorrows and love. You were secure with the knowledge of your value to your family. We surrounded you, loved you, and watched you very gently go into eternal rest and peace. You would not suffer discomfort any longer. And we all wept.

A passing neighbor saw what was happening and delivered a card with white sage to burn and dried forget-me-nots. A dear friend sent me a book. The next day a lifelong friend delivered to my children a poem (see below) to which I attached "Bear"'s last photo.

I miss my "Bear." But I visit his grave under the aspen tree frequently. And I still have heart-to-heart conversations with him. I will always love him. No other dog will ever replace him. But another dog could enlighten my life. I am not ready yet; grieving takes time for me.

Dogs teach us many lessons about life, which can be too frightening for us to understand otherwise. Dogs teach about unconditional love and trust. Perhaps if we could learn to trust and love each other with such consistency, the world would be a better place.

Thank you, "Bear," for being my teacher. I will never forget you — never!

"Phoebe"

by Barbara Trachtenberg

I found the litter in an alley behind a sewing machine shop in Manhattan Beach California. After several visits and lots of pleading, I finally convinced my husband that we should get two puppies. This was about a year after the loss of "Brows," our 14-year-old family dog. I felt that our empty house had been quiet long enough.

Stan and I went to choose our new family members. He picked a rambunctious, stocky male who was gnawing at his shoelaces. I chose a sweet, quiet, small female who was observing her littermates and "smiling" at me. "Holden" and "Phoebe" instantly became a part of our life. I loved it. Each morning we got up and ran, socialized with the neighbors, and explored our worlds together.

"Phoebe" worshiped Stan. She ran up to him when he got home and wiggled her entire body in joy. This worked in her favor as it lessened his annoyance at a giant hole chewed in one of our carpets and a large round hole gnawed in the service porch wall. And "Holden" followed me everywhere.

The bottom line was that "Holden" and "Phoebe" adored each other. They were a team. If we clicked our tongues to get their attention they would cock their heads at exactly the same moment. If we got them dog biscuits, they would sit and look at us with the same longing in their eyes. They spent countless hours running around the house and yard, playing and getting into trouble. They were always taking care of each other. "Phoebe" never let us touch her eyes to clean them but she would lie back and let "Holden" lick them clean for her. To us they became "HoldenPhoebe," a new word in our vocabulary.

You can imagine our distress when "Phoebe," who had been coughing and losing weight, was diagnosed with cardiomyopathy, a condition that enlarges the heart and weakens the heart muscle. We were told that there was no cure for this condition and that at best she would have a couple of months to live; it didn't seem possible. We had just taken a lively walk up Snow King the day before and my vet was surprised that "Phoebe" had the energy to get in and out of the car.

"Phoebe" began to get sicker but she never lost her spirit. I made a conscious decision that I would rather she "die with her boots on" and enjoy the last months of her life than keep her quiet and inside. Every day we went to the river. "Holden," unaware, would run and socialize while "Phoebe" would try to keep up but then drop back to walk quietly by my side. I eventually dragged a sled behind us to haul her if she got too tired to walk.

I knew that the time had come when "Phoebe" could no longer lie down at night due to discomfort. One evening she wandered out the dog door when it was 25 degrees below zero. She didn't know where she was because she wasn't getting enough oxygen to her brain. Had I not heard her go outside I am afraid that she might have frozen to death. The next morning we called the family together to say goodbye. I knew that we couldn't let her go on like that any more.

The loss was devastating. "Phoebe"'s kissing and wiggling had started our mornings with a smile. "Holden" was confused. At first he thought that she had just gone to the vet and he enjoyed the attention that we showered on him. Little by little, as he, and we, realized that "Phoebe" was not coming back, he became despondent. He lost his spark, lying down all day by the front door, waiting for the return of his best friend, his sister. His spirit dwindled. When we took him for his favorite walk up Cache Creek, he would obediently follow us, making little or no attempt to play with other dogs. "Holden" was sad; our house was sad.

Although it had been a relatively short time, "Holden" was so depressed that I decided to try to find a puppy. My rationale was that "Holden" needed a companion. I had to tell myself that we were not replacing "Phoebe" as no other dog could do that for either "Holden" or us. Maybe I was jumping into this too quickly and we should wait awhile to give us all a chance to adjust. In the end, we decided to find a puppy. It took several weeks but we finally found a puppy who stole our hearts.

We brought her home and introduced her to "Holden." He showed average interest in her at first but she was persistent. She thought "Holden" was her mother and constantly snuggled up to him and loved him. He began to enjoy the attention and his spirits perked up. He started to play with her and eventually with other dogs again. "Holly" has wormed her way into our lives and our hearts and we love her for her unique spirit and personality.

One of the more significant moments through this whole experience happened at the vet's office about a week after we got "Holly." I had taken her in for a checkup. On my way out someone in the office asked me to wait a moment. "Phoebe"'s ashes had just arrived from Idaho Falls and she wanted me to take them home. I walked out of the office with "Phoebe"'s ashes in one hand and my brand new puppy in the other. "There has to be a message in this," I said as I smiled and got into my car.

Three in a Row
by Judy F. Eddy

Having to euthanize our three beloved dogs in three years was no easy matter. In fact, it was heartbreaking.

"BJ" went first. Our black Labrador, sweeter than smart, was "mommy's boy." He had been found in a laundromat when he was about 2-1/2 months old and we were fortunate to be able to adopt him from the animal shelter to keep our "Poppy" company. "Poppy" was also from the animal shelter, a puppy we adopted to enliven our home because we knew our 15-year-old "Lady" would not live for too long (and she died about two months later). "Poppy," a golden/setter mix, was sweet and intelligent. Both dogs readily let us take into our home "Inyo," our daughter's Weimaraner.

All three dogs ran with us every day, and because of "BJ"'s background, he never left our side — being lost once was enough for him. "Poppy" was an eternal puppy — bouncing and leaping, rubbing her cheeks on my knees after her meal and then, without fail, giving me her best — a loud burp! When "Inyo" came to live with us, all three dogs were approximately five years old. He had no problem accepting "Poppy" as mistress of the pack. The three of them were best friends and were always together.

"BJ" had thyroid problems, arthritis, and ear problems. When it all became too much for him to bear and his quality of life was nonexistent, our vet came to the house and while the other two dogs were outside, we sobbed, holding him as he breathed his last. We wrapped him in a blanket and he was buried in a pre-dug hole while I kept "Poppy" and "Inyo" as close to me as possible. They knew I was crying but they didn't know why. We planted an evergreen for "BJ."

The following year, "Poppy" was diagnosed with cancer but surgery couldn't remove all of it. Although she was in remission, her missing us while we were in Washington DC with Clinton's healthcare taskforce could trigger it again. It was extremely difficult for us to have "Poppy" euthanized because she was so energetic (although we knew it was only temporary) and there was no way to know when she would die. Our vet was so caring, not commenting on how hard we were crying, not making us feel foolish because we could not stop the tears. Because we knew about "Poppy"'s cancer, we had her hole dug before the winter snows froze the soil. Covered with a tarp, it was ready for her. Another tree in the spring -- now it was two years and two dogs!

"Inyo" was alone but he did not grieve too much, with all the attention he got as our "only" dog. But the next year he developed epilepsy and medicine helped only temporarily. One "fit" left him so paralyzed that he could no longer stand or walk; he had to be carried outside and held to empty his bladder. He could not understand what had happened to him and we knew that his time had come. Again, the vet came to our home and again he watched as we cradled our last dog and let the tears gush forth. And a third tree covers the spot where our third dog is buried.

After 34 years of raising children and dogs, I needed a break — I did not want another dog; I wanted the freedom of no responsibilities. But it became apparent that I could not live without a dog in my life. Six months later, "Toby," another Weimaraner, became a part of the family.

Within two months my husband left me and all I had was "Toby." However, he was enough! Not only was he a handful, requiring much time and attention, he was the reason I had to get out every day to face the world when I'd rather be inside feeling sorry for myself. Because of him and his extreme friendliness toward people, I started Teton County PAL. Because of him, PAWS of Jackson Hole is in existence. And because of "Toby," I can face life with strength, knowing that I will always have his love for as long as he lives. When he is gone, his memories might suffice. But I know that I will always have dogs in my heart, if not in my home.

"The one best place to bury a good dog is in the heart of his master."
Ben Hur Lampman

Dearest Family

"I explained it to St Peter,
I'd rather stay here just outside the Pearly Gates.
I won't be a nuisance; I won't bark.
I'll just lie here and wait, no matter how long you might be.
I'll be here just gnawing on a celestial bone,
Watching for celestial bird.
I'd miss you so much if I went in alone.
It just wouldn't be Heaven to me without all of you."

Love from "Bear," June 14 1999

If it Should Be

If it should be I grow frail and weak
And pain prevents my peaceful sleep,
Then you must do what must be done
When this last battle can t be won.
You will be sad, I understand,
Selfishness might stay your hand.
But on this day, more than the rest,
Your love and friendship take the test.
We ve had so many happy years
That what s to come can hold no fears.
You d not want me to suffer,
So when the time comes, please let me go.
Take me where my needs they ll tend;
Only   stay with me until the end.
Hold me firm and speak to me
Until my eyes no longer see.
I know, in time, you too will see
It is a kindness that you do for me.
Although my tail its last has waved,
From pain and suffering I ve been saved.
Do not grieve it should be you
Who must decide this thing to do.
We ve been so close, we two, these years...
Don t let your heart hold any tears.

Author unknown

Heaven Knows

A man and his dog were walking along a road. The man was enjoying the scenery when it suddenly occurred to him that he was dead. He remembered dying, and that his dog had been dead for years. He wondered where the road was leading them. After awhile, they came to a high, white stone wall along one side of the road. It looked like fine marble.

At the top of a long hill, the wall was broken by a tall arch that glowed in the sunlight. When he was standing before it, he saw a magnificent gate in the arch that looked like mother of pearl, and the street that led to the gate looked like pure gold. He and the dog walked toward the gate and as he got closer, he saw a man at a desk to one side. When he was close enough, he called out, 'Excuse me, where are we?"

"This is heaven, sir," the man answered.

"Wow! Would you happen to have some water?" The man asked.

"Of course, sir. Come right in, and I'll have some ice water brought right away."

The man gestured and the gate began to open.

"Can my friend," gesturing toward his dog, "come in, too?" the traveler asked.

"I'm sorry, sir, but we don't accept pets."

The man thought a moment and then turned back toward the road and continued the way he had been going. After another long walk, and at the top of another long hill, he came to a dirt road that led through a farm gate that looked as if it had never been closed. There was no fence. As he approached the gate, he saw a man inside, leaning against a tree and reading a book.

"Excuse me!" he called to the reader. "Do you have any water?"

"Year, sure, there's a pump over there." The man pointed to a place that couldn't be seen from outside the gate. "Come on in."

"How about my friend here?" The traveler gestured to his dog.

"There should be a bowl by the pump."

They went through the gate, and sure enough, there was an old-fashioned handpump with a bowl beside it. The traveler filled the bowl and took a long drink for himself and then he gave some to the dog. When they were no longer thirsty, he and his dog walked back toward the man who was standing by the tree waiting for them.

"What do you call this place?" the traveler asked.

"This is heaven," was the answer.

"Well, that's confusing," the traveler said. "The man down the road said that was heaven, too."

"Oh, you mean the place with the gold street and pearly gates? Nope. That's hell."

"Doesn't it make you mad for them to use your name like that?"

"No. I can see how you might think so but we're just happy that they screen out the folks who will leave their best friends behind."

The Rainbow Bridge

There is a bridge connecting Heaven and Earth. It is called the Rainbow Bridge because of its many colors. Just this side of the Rainbow Bridge there is a land of meadows, hills and valleys with lush green grass.

When a beloved pet dies, the pet goes to this place. There is always food and water and warm spring weather. The old and frail animals are young again. Those who are maimed are made whole again. They play with each other all day long.

There is only one thing missing; they are not with their special person who loved them on Earth. So, each day they run and play until the day comes when one suddenly stops playing and looks up. The nose twitches. The ears are up. The eyes are staring. And this one suddenly runs from the group!

You have been seen, and when you and your special friend meet, you take him or her in your arms and embrace. Your face is kissed again and again and you look once more in the eyes of your trusting pet.

Then you cross the Rainbow Bridge together, never again to be separated.

Author unknown

Every Cloud Has A Silver Lining

My best friend closed his eyes last night
As his head was in my hand.
The doctors said he was in pain
And it was hard for him to stand.
The thoughts that scurried through my head
As I cradled him in my arms
Were of his younger puppy years,
And oh! his many charms.
Today, there was no gentle nudge
With an intense "I love you" gaze,
Only a heart that's filled with tears,
Remembering our joy-filled days.
But an angel just appeared to me
And he said, "You should cry no more.
God loves our canine friends;
He's installed a doggie door."

Author unknown

You've Gone to the Dogs When ...

- Your dog is the star of your World Wide Web site
- You carry pictures of your dog in your wallet instead of pictures of your children, parents, siblings, significant other, or anyone else remotely human
- You make popcorn just to play catch with your dog
- You keep eating even after finding a dog hair in your pasta
- You avoid vacuuming the house as long as possible because your dog is afraid of the vacuum cleaner
- You shovel a zigzag path in the back yard snow so your dog can reach all his favorite spots
- You never completely finish a piece of steak or chicken so your dog can get a taste, too
- Your freezer contains more dog bones than anything else
- You keep an extra water dish in your second-floor bedroom, in case your dog gets thirsty at night (after all, her other dish is way down on the first floor...)
- Your weekend activities are planned around taking your dog for a hike (both days)
- Your friend's dog acts as Best Dog at your wedding
- Your parents refer to your pet as their granddog
- You don't go to happy hours with coworkers anymore because you need to go home and see your dog
- You have a kiddie wading pool in the yard but no small children
- You have baby gates permanently installed at strategic places around the house, but no babies
- The trashbasket is more or less permanently installed in the kitchen sink to keep the dog out of it while you're at work
- You can't see out the passenger side of the windshield because there are noseprints all over the inside
- Poop has become a source of conversation for you and your significant other
- You refer to yourselves as Mommy and Daddy
- Your dog sleeps with you
- You have 32 different names for your dog; most make no sense but he understands
- You'd rather stay home on Saturday night and cuddle your dog than go to the movies with your sweetie
- You go to the pet supply store every Saturday because it's one of the very few places that lets you bring your dog inside and your dog loves to go with you

- You open your purse and that big bunch of baggies you use for pickups pops out
- You get an extra-long hose on your shower-massage just so you can use it to wash your dog in the tub without making the dog sit hip-deep in water
- You don't think it's the least bit strange to stand in the back-yard chirping, "Fido, pee!" over and over again while Fido tends to play and forget what he's out there for (what your neighbors thinks of your behavior is yet another story)
- You and the dog come down with something like the flu on the same day
- Your dog sees the veterinarian while you settle for an over-the-counter remedy from the drugstore
- Your dog is getting old and arthritic so you buy lumber and build her a small staircase so she can climb onto the bed by herself
- Your license plate or license plate frame mentions your dog
- You match your furniture/carpet/clothes to your dog
- You have your dog's picture on your office desk (but no one else's)
- You lecture people on responsible dog ownership every chance you get
- You hang around the dog section of your local bookstore
- You skip breakfast so you can walk your dog in the morning before work
- You are the only idiot walking in the pouring rain because your dog needs his walk
- Nobody's feet are allowed on the furniture but your dogs are welcome to sleep on any piece they choose
- It takes an entirely separate garbage can to handle the poop
- All kinds of things around the house are in need of repair but the injured dog you rescued by the side of the road requires immediate surgery and out comes the checkbook
- You and your family haven't had your annual checkup in two years but the dogs are all medically up to date
- You start barking at your children to "Sit! Stay!"
- You're more concerned with the dogs' needs than your own when the budget gets tight
- At least three of your five weeks' vacation are scheduled around grooming, vaccinations and dental cleaning ... all for the dogs
- Dog crates double as chairs and/or tables in your family room
- You can remember people only by associating them with their dog
- Overnight guests (who share your bed) are offended by having to sleep with you and the dog(s)

- You snuggle closer to the dog than the person with whom you are sleeping
- You decide to downsize from a huge house in the city to an average country cottage with lots of land in order to build the kennel of your dreams
- You spend more time looking through mailorder catalogues for dog supplies than for Victoria's Secret nighties or Miles Kimball gadgets
- All your social activities revolve around other dog people
- Your voice is recognized by your veterinarian's receptionist
- Everyone at the office is eager to know if the dogs are all right because you were late for the meeting
- The whereabouts of all your important legal and personal documents escapes you, yet you know precisely where to locate the file that includes all the veterinarian records, breed papers and registration
- Your trunk has an emergency food kit for any strays you might come across
- The majority of your charitable contributions go to animal organizations
- To win a precious $0.75 show ribbon, you think nothing of forking out hundreds of dollars to board/pet sit the other dogs, pay for entry fees, gas, accommodations and meals
- You no longer have to buy extra large garbage bags because the empty 40-pound dog food bags work just as well
- Complete strangers call you on the phone to ask questions because they heard you were a "dog person"
- Every gift you ever get has something to do with dogs
- Your cookie jar has never seen the likes of people cookies
- You rip up the carpet and lay tile to make cleanup so much easier
- Your family complains that you always take more pictures of the dog than you do of them
- While proudly showing off your family album, your guest asks, "Isn't there anyone else in your family beside the dog?"
- Any conversation you're having is effortlessly directed back to the topic of dogs
- Your first concern when planning a vacation is whether the hotel will take pets
- You politely bow out of an important social engagement so you can attend a dog show
- The number one priority when buying a new house is the size and landscape of the backyard
- The only (or at least first) forum you log onto is the animal forum

- You describe your children as having temperaments rather than personalities
- The cost of boarding your furkids equals that of your entire vacation
- Your dog decides he doesn't like someone and you tend to agree
- All your nondog friends know to dress down when visiting your house
- Your friends know which chair not to sit in
- First-time visitors wonder aloud: "Do you smell something?" and you really don't
- You become the family dog kennel for all your relatives
- You don't think twice about sitting on the floor because both the couch and the chair are completely dog full
- Your desk proudly displays your canine family
- All dates must pass your dog's inspection
- The first question you ask when on a date is: "So, do you like animals?"
- You buy a bigger bed that will comfortably sleep six
- You break down and buy another pillow so you can have one to sleep on
- More than half your grocery money goes to dog food and treats
- You buy a mini-van to give them all enough travel room
- Your carpeting matches the color of your dog — purposely
- The thought of changing a baby's diaper makes you swoon but you can pick up dog poop barehanded, if necessary, without batting an eye
- You send out specially-made holiday cards that feature you and the dogs
- Your significant other issues the ultimatum: "It's them or me!" and you have no problem pointing out the suitcase
- You readily allow your dogs to give you slobbery kisses, but you don't dare wipe a toddler's nose
- Onlookers grimace at the sight of you sharing your sandwich with your four-legged pal, bite for bite
- Your dog has the best birthday party over and above any kid in the entire neighborhood
- Your dogs eat only the most nutritionally sound food while your favorite meal is macaroni and cheese
- You've traced your dog's family tree further than you have your own
- You're more familiar with dog laws than you are with people laws
- Your veterinarian's office number is the first one on your speed dial list; his home is number two

- You stagger your dog magazine subscriptions to make sure you'll receive one every week
- One of your veterinarian files is labeled "Other"
- You can't remember family birthdays and anniversaries, but you can rattle off a six-generation pedigree with birthdate, health data and coat colors at the drop of a hat
- Your veterinarian takes a few extra courses just to keep up with your breed's assorted ailments
- You have two dog doors between the house and the fenced yard so the doggies can run circles, half inside, half outside
- You rush to get home from work in time to get some of what your spouse is fixing for the dogs since s/he doesn't cook for you
- You've just spent $60 on groceries and realize none of it is for yourself
- Your file is the only one that remains in the "IN" box at the veterinarian's office
- Anyone can look at your (pick all that apply) — t-shirt, sweatshirt, coffee mug, keychain, beach towel, cooking apron, couch throw, tote bag, computer screen saver/wallpaper/mousepad/wristpad/monitor frame, gift wrapping paper, photographic displays, calendars, refrigerator magnets, weathervane, doormat, bumper stickers, umbrella, Christmas sweater, socks, embroidery project, child's collection of stuffed animals, sheets and bedspreads, checks, checkbook covers, throw pillows, Home Pages, — and know immediately that you are a dog lover, AND probably what particular breed you favor
- Your bedspread doesn't have to coordinate with the bedroom because it's always covered with a sheet for the dogs anyway; ditto for the couches
- Your veterinarian file rivals *War and Peace*
- The family's eye doctor is located in town but the dog's ophthalmologist is located a two-hour drive away
- Your medications are available at the drugstore down the block but your dog's medication has to be ordered from and shipped by a specialist
- It's easier to get a hairdresser's appointment for yourself than it is to get one for your dog
- Dog hair in food is just another spice
- Your dogs have their own Christmas card and gift list, and they receive cards and gifts in return
- Your dogs have their own Christmas tree, and it's so full of ornaments that they need a larger one

- The part of your will dealing with your dogs is longer than any other part
- The guardians of your dogs will receive a larger amount of insurance policy money than will all other members of your family, combined
- The instructions to the people at the dog kennel are longer than the instructions to the house sitter
- Your personal library is heavy on dog books, and so is the library for which you order books
- Your favorite month is April, National Dog Appreciation Month
- Your dogs have a larger wardrobe of holiday-related bandanas than you do
- You hate to go to the grocery store for people food but when the dog treats are gone, off you go with no hesitation, even at the busiest time
- You have three Home Pages, all of them dealing with your dogs, your friends' dogs, your dogs' friends, etc.
- The most exciting times on vacations, no matter where in the world you go, is when you get to pet a dog (a "canine fix")
- Most of your vacation pictures are of dogs around the world
- The largest display of collectibles in the house is dog stuff — plates, photos, cards, etc.
- You kiss your dog more than 10 times per greeting
- You introduce your dog to the photographer and ask, "Would you like to kiss Fido also?"
- You cut your vacations to 3-day weekends only
- You call long distance and talk with your dog
- You order 250 Christmas photos of just the dog with no family in the photos
- You order 5x7 photos of the kids and order 16x20 photos of Spot
- Your Mother's Day (birthday, anniversary, etc.) present is a puppy
- The only time you use your camper is for dog shows
- The part of the backyard you finish first is the dog run
- You spend more time on the computer dealing with "dog stuff" than with "other stuff"
- Your "Welcome" sign has a dog on it
- Your email address is your kennel name
- Your dog eats cat poop but you still let her kiss you (not immediately afterward, of course)
- You like people who like your dog; you despise people who don't
- Your carry dog biscuits in your purse or pocket at all times

- You talk about your dog the way other people talk about their kid
- You sign and send birthday/anniversary/Christmas cards from your dog
- You put an extra blanket on the bed so your dog can be comfortable
- Your dog's toybox has more toys in it than does that of your children
- You bank where your dog gets a biscuit at the driveup
- You purchase automobile fuel at the station where the attendant gives your dog a biscuit
- If you recognize yourself in 90% or more of these, then you *really have* gone to the dogs!

Doggie Dictionary

BATH — A process by which the humans drench the floor, walls and themselves. You can help by shaking vigorously and frequently.

BICYCLE — A two-wheeled exercise machine, invented for dogs to control body fat. To get maximum aerobic benefit, you must hide behind a bush and dash out, bark loudly and run alongside for a few yards. The person then swerves and falls into the bushes and you prance away.

BUMP — The best way to get your humans' attention when they are drinking a fresh cup of coffee or tea.

DEAFNESS — A malady that affects dogs when their person wants them in and they want to stay out. Symptoms include staring blankly at the person and then running in the opposite direction, or lying down.

DOG BED — Any soft, clean surface, such as the white bedspread in the guest room or the newly upholstered couch in the living room.

DROOL — What you do when your persons have food and you don't. To do this properly you must sit as close as you can and look sad. Let the drool fall to the floor, or better yet, onto their laps.

FORCE-FETCH — When you drop the toy under the furniture, scratch at the carpet until your person is forced to "fetch" it.

GARBAGE CAN — A container that your neighbors put out once a week to test your ingenuity. You must stand on your hind legs and try to push the lid off with your nose. If you do it right, you are rewarded with margarine wrappers to shred, beef bones to consume, and moldy crusts of bread to munch.

GOOSE BUMP — A maneuver to use as a last resort when the regular BUMP doesn't get the attention you require. It is especially effective when combined with the SNIFF.

LEAN — Every good dog's response to the command, "Sit!" especially if your person is dressed for an evening out; it is incredibly effective before black-tie events.

LEASH — A strap that attaches to your collar, enabling you to lead your person where you want him or her to go.

LOVE — A feeling of intense affection, given freely and without restriction. The best way you can show your love is to wag your tail. If you are lucky, a human will love you in return.

PEDIGREE — Dog food with lots of great coupons to encourage your person to buy more.

SNIFF — A social custom to use when you greet other dogs.

SOFA — An item of furniture that is to dogs like napkins are to people. After eating, it is polite to run up and down the front of the sofa and wipe your whiskers clean.

THUNDER — A signal that the world is coming to an end. Humans remain amazingly calm during thunderstorms so it is necessary to warn them of the danger by trembling uncontrollably, panting, rolling your eyes wildly, and following at their heels.

WASTEBASKET — A dog toy filled with paper, envelopes, and old candy wrappers. When you get bored, turn the basket over and strew the papers all over the house until your person comes home.

About the Authors

Editor JUDY F. EDDY, has loved dogs since childhood, and has always been owned by at least one. She founded Teton County PAL, a Pet Partner program in Teton County that promotes the animal-human bond, because of her wonderful Weimaraner's ("Toby") extreme friendliness and love for people. Judy and Toby make a Pet Partner® team. Judy is President of the Board of Directors of Teton County PAL. She also writes a highly acclaimed quarterly newsletter for the Pet Partners® and the community. Judy is a founding member of PAWS of Jackson Hole and is the current President of that organization as well. A health policy researcher, her first love is dogs. Judy is currently working on several animal-related projects, including getting her certification from FEMA for the care of "Animals in Disasters."

JUSTIN ADAMS comes from Virginia. He has hunted birds with his dogs (Brittany spaniels and English pointers, English springer spaniels, and English setters) for 40 of his 50 years. According to Justin, hunting birds without dogs is a lot worse than dinner without wine or a day without sunshine.

LORENE BAGLEY writes: "One fantastic thing about dogs is that they are always happy to share my hobbies without a bit of complaint — hiking, skiing, running, and sometimes birding ... if I can get Chief to quiet down while I observe the abundance of species flying around our wonderful mountains. Chief has come to mean all that and more. He came to me at a time when he was the ONLY constant good I could see. He was always "golden" — always loved me ... always glad to see me. But most important, he was the one who was ALWAYS there when I needed him. This bond has grown with each day. Chief renewed my faith in love."

JAKE ELKINS has been on the Jackson Hole Ski Patrol since 1977 and currently is the Assistant Patrol Director and Canine Coordinator at the Jackson Hole Mountain Resort. He has owned and handled three avalanche dogs, all golden retrievers. "Barley Corn" was the second avalanche rescue dog on the patrol. She worked for 10 years and at 16 years of age, was able to enjoy a retirement that included crosscountry skiing, hiking, fishing, pheasant hunting, and lots of sofa time before she went to her final rest. "Worker Corn," while on the patrol for only four years (she died of cancer), was validated by the Canadian Avalanche Rescue Dog Association for her performance in their Advanced Course. Jake is currently handling "Pepper Corn," and at one year of age she was already locating multiple (volunteer) victims who are buried in snow to a depth of five feet.

TERRIE FAIR is a Program Assistant with the Teton County/Jackson Parks and Recreation Department. One of the most exciting and fun events that she conducts for the dogs in Jackson is the Alpo Canine Frisbee Competition. A dog lover and dog owner most of her life, Terrie thinks that it is great to see both dog and owner participating together in such a fun activity.

RON KIEHN has always loved pets. His oldest son got his first Labrador retriever in 1968 and Ron has always had one or more Labradors since. He started in field trials in the late 1980s. One of his hardest jobs is placing those who are not of championship caliber into a proper home. He might sell one if he is convinced it will be living at a very good home for a hunting dog. He presently has a great dog, "Westwind Lone Runner," who has just passed his twelfth birthday. This dog has completely lost his hearing but he still loves the water and he loves to retrieve.

MARGIE LYNCH is the Executive Director of Friends of Pathways, a nonprofit organization that seeks to enhance nonmotorized transportation and recreation options in Jackson Hole. Margie moved to Jackson Hole in 1996 to escape her life as an overworked Washington DC lawyer. She enjoys walking, bicycling and crosscountry skiing on the Pathways, and is often accompanied in these activities by her friends' canine companions.

JUANITA MCGHEE writes: "As long as I can remember, I have had a love affair with animals, especially dogs and horses. During my school years, I frequently coaxed stray dogs home with me. Because of this, I was able to learn about numerous breeds and loved them all. I also read and devoured all the Albert Payson Terhune dog books about his Sunnybank collies and dreamed of having a collie of my own. When this became a reality, I showed my collies in AKC obedience and conformation classes. They have earned many awards in various shows, but even more, have been great companions and enjoy visiting schools and nursing homes. I love all the activities that provide opportunities to do things with dogs. That is one reason I have been a 4-H dog leader for many years. It is great being involved with both the young owners and their dogs. It is also why I am proud to belong to Teton County PAL."

CORIE RYBAK moved to Jackson in 1984 after graduating from the University of Vermont, and has worked as a legal assistant and Forest Service Ranger. For 14 years she had many memorable experiences exploring many of the hiking trails described in this book with her canine companion Zeb, the wonder mutt, until age caught up with him in 1997. That same fall, Corie assumed the responsibilities as manager of the Jackson/Teton County Animal Shelter. An advocate for the well-being of all animals, she cares for impounded dogs and cats, finds homes for adoptable pets, assists in the enforcement of animal regulations, and educates the public about responsible pet care.

SANDY STROUT, President of the Jackson Hole Kennel Club, a grassroots organization, started dog training for the Club in 1981 when she moved to Jackson. When Sandy watched Rin Tin Tin, she decided that she wanted a German shepherd. Sandy has been addicted to the breed ever since and now owns 3 shepherds. Backpacking, hiking and traveling are never without the dogs. Sandy spent several years showing in the AKC Obedience ring, and took one dog through Utility. She began to give obedience classes about 20 years ago. She feels joy when she can communicate to others how to "listen" to their animals, and how to foster good interpersonal skills to help animals be a part of the family. Sandy trains dogs, rescues and places animals, rides horses, and learns something new about animals every day.

OATSY VON GONTARD is a native of Jackson Hole, growing up on her family's cattle ranch in South Park. Her constant companions were dogs and horses. Oatsy was certified as a Master Trainer for canines at the top of her class in Ohio. She worked for Canine Companions for Independence in Santa Rosa California, training dogs to assist people with disabilities. Currently, she trains with professional gun dog trainer Kean Bailey, along with teaching obedience, puppy preschool, agility, and just about any other canine-related activity.

TRACY WALKER was the Executive Director of the Teton Valley Humane Society in Driggs, Idaho. Her love for animals is evidenced by her continuing work with the TVHS.

JANET WILTS has been a National Park Ranger for 20 years and has helped with search and rescue in Yellowstone and Grand Teton National Parks, as well as at Point Reyes and Whiskeytown. She is currently a Jenny Lake Climbing Ranger. Janet started working with search dogs in 1988. Since then, she has certified three of her own dogs and has helped train numerous others. She was president of Jackson Hole Search Dogs for two years. She is currently the Testing and Training Officer of Wyoming K-9 SAR. She has also taught SAR dog strategy for beginning groups in Arizona and Wyoming.

Index

A

B

C